EASY
GLUTEN FREE DESSERTS

Gluten Free Cakes, Bake From Scratch Cookies and Biscuits, Killer Pancakes, Wicked Good Cupcakes and Muffins, AIP Recipes, Celiac Disease Diet Treats, and more

Milica Vladova
"Easy Gluten Free Desserts: Gluten Free Cakes, Bake From Scratch Cookies and Biscuits, Killer Pancakes, Wicked Good Cupcakes and Muffins, AIP Recipes, Celiac Disease Diet Treats, and more"

Copyright © 2018 by Militsa Vladova

FREE EBOOKS

Strengthen your immunity, detox, energize, heal, and stimulate your metabolism with these magical potent healthy recipes!

Get your FREE copy of
"10 Powerful Immune Boosting Recipes"
"12 Healthy Dessert Recipes"
"15 Delicious & Healthy Smoothies"
"The Complete Ayurveda Detox"

Go to *www.MindBodyAndSpiritWellbeing.com* and claim your book!

Or simply scan the QR code below:

Dedicated to all the people battling with chronic diseases every single day!

You are true heroes!

Contents

Introduction

The gluten-free diet has been considered to be the latest fashion in the health and wellness industries. It is often ridiculed, frowned-upon, and not taken seriously.

But does this relatively new nutritional plan deserve this attitude?

In my humble opinion – definitely not! And not just because I consider myself part of these industries, but because I have seen and felt the detrimental effects of gluten on my own body and mind!

I have been suffering from irritable bowel syndrome (IBS) for many years. For as long as I can remember, I have been constantly bloated, experiencing severe pain and discomfort in my intestines, constipation, inflated guts pressing my ovaries, and moodiness.

Needless to say, I have been jumping from one doctor to another, and they all could not solve this puzzle.

The usual IBS protocol excludes most of the fiber and gassy foods from the diet, such as legumes, fresh fruits and vegetables, seeds, etc. And what was recommended for me was eating mostly toasted bread and soft creamy meals.

Yeah, been there, done that! Did it work? No.

So, what has been causing all these discomforts?

Thankfully, my own sensible and caring GP suggested I made a diary of everything I eat and test out which foods trigger the bloating one by one.

My discovery was very surprising – it was bread – white bread packed with gluten!

And as soon as I removed it from my menu and substituted it with gluten-free foods or products which were very low on this wheat protein (like einkorn and emmer), the discomforts disappeared into thin air! It happened so quickly, it was almost unbelievable to me!

Now I can imagine what people with severe gluten intolerance have to go through every single day!

So, for me – the gluten sensitivity is not a myth, it is not a fabrication of the food industries, it's not the latest nutritional hipster fashion – it is a real threat!

And sadly, it is a possible threat not just to those with celiac disease, but to all of us!

The gluten intolerance can emerge out of nowhere at any point in our lives without a notice. Because most of us experience the negative effects of this protein on a daily basis without even realizing it! Bloating, meteorism (painful gassiness), constipation, food allergies, skin issues (like psoriasis, eczemas), depression, mood swings, ADHD, dementia, and so on and so on...

More than 55 diseases and ailments have been linked to the regular consumption of gluten!

Why is that? What happened to our gluten tolerance? Why didn't our ancestors have any issues with it?

The answer is very simple – the wheat grains are extremely genetically modified nowadays, so that the percentage of gluten in them has risen from 5% to the whooping 50%! Yes, half of the wheat we eat consists of this allergy causing protein! And as you may know – all allergen foods taken in large quantities for a long period of time can unlock a sensitivity or a food intolerance. So, take it as a time bomb that can go off any minute!

That is why I decided to write this book and help people start making better nutritional choices!

And because most of us have a sweet tooth, my first gluten-free volume will be focused on healthy desserts – pies, pancakes, cakes, cookies, brownies, etc.

The aim of this book is to make your life easier and the lives of all those who must stay away from this wheat protein for the sake of their health:

> People suffering from **celiac disease**;
> Those with **gluten sensitivity** and intolerance;
> **Irritable bowel syndrome** (IBS);
> **Autoimmune disorders** (Hashimoto, lupus, psoriasis, arthritis);
> **Mental issues** (depression, anxiety, OCD, ADHD, dementia, Alzheimer's disease);
> And **anyone** who wants to test the gluten-free lifestyle and see if their well-being and energy levels would improve!

Of course, I feel the need to point out that should you suffer from any ailment, do not hesitate to consult with your doctor or nutritionist to determine which foods would be best for you to consume (or avoid) for your particular case!

I know you are here for the recipes!
So, let's get cooking!

GLUTEN-FREE PANCAKES AND CREPES

Pancakes

Ingredients:

3 Tbsps. **Rice flour**
2 Tbsps. **Corn flour** (non-GMO)
2 Tbsps. **Coconut flour**
2 Tbsps. **Desiccated coconut**
1 **Egg**
1 Tbsp. **Coconut butter** (melted)
1 tsp. **Coconut sugar**
A pinch of **Salt**
A pinch of **Baking soda**
Some **Water**

Instructions:

Whisk the egg in a cup.

In a large bowl, mix the rice flour, corn flour, desiccated coconut, the sugar, salt, and the baking soda. Mix the ingredients well to blend them.

Next, add the egg and the coconut butter. Stir again nicely.

Now start slowly adding water while stirring. The goal is to reach the consistency of pancake batter – semi-liquid. Blend the ingredients once again with a hand mixer to break down any lumps.

Heat a frying pan and cover it with some coconut oil/butter. Bake the pancakes as usual.

Tapioca Pancakes

Ingredients:

1 Egg
1/2 cup **Milk**
A pinch of **Salt**
1/4 tsp. **Vanilla powder** (or liquid extract)
2 Tbsps. **Tapioca flour**
2 Tbsps. **Coconut butter** (melted)

Instructions:

Blend the ingredients well with a hand mixer.

Adjust the quantities of the flour or milk to reach the desired consistency, if you need to.

Bake the pancakes in a non-stick pan.

Note: the pancakes are very gentle, so you may need to grease the pan. Also be very careful when flipping them – they can easily break.

My notes:

Rice Pancakes

Ingredients:

1 cup **Rice flour**
1 cup **Milk**
1 **Egg**
1 Tbsp. **Maple syrup** (or agave)
2 Tbsps. **Olive oil**
2 tsps. **Baking powder**
A pinch of **Salt**

Instructions:

Place the flour in a large bowl. Add the baking powder, the salt, and the maple syrup. Mix well to blend the ingredients.

Next, add the milk and stir again.

In another container, beat the egg, and transfer it to the flour along with the olive oil.

Whisk the batter to fully homogenize it.

Bake the pancakes as usual in a hot non-stick pan on each side.

Garnish with maple syrup, honey, or your favorite sugar-free jam.

American Rice Pancakes

Ingredients:

2 cups **Rice flour**
2 cups **Coconut milk**
2 **Eggs**
2 tsps. **Agave syrup**
4 Tbsps. **Olive oil**
4 tsps. **Baking powder**

Instructions:

The process is the same as the most common pancake recipes.

Place the rice flour in a large bowl. Add the baking powder and the agave syrup. Mix them well.

Next, pour the milk and stir until you blend the ingredients completely.

In another container, whisk the eggs, and add them to the pancake batter along with the olive oil.

Blend the mixture one last time to reach a homogenous mass.

Bake the pancakes in a hot pan on each side.

My notes:

Fiber Pancakes with Psyllium Husk

Ingredients:

3 Tbsps. **Coconut flour**
1 tsp. **Psyllium husk**
2 Tbsps. **Yogurt**
2 **Eggs**

Instructions:

Simply blend all the ingredients well and bake the pancakes in a hot pan.

Simple as that!

My notes:

Gluten-free Pancakes with Tahini

Ingredients:

2 Tbsps. **Gluten-free flour mix of choice**
2 **Eggs**
1 tsp. **Ground flax seeds**
1 Tbsp. **Sesame tahini**
1 **Banana**
Some **Fresh berries** (strawberries, blueberries, raspberries, etc.) - optional
Some **Desiccated coconut** - optional

Instructions:

The process is similar to any kind on pancakes.

Beat the eggs in a large cup and blend them with the flax seeds, and the flour.

Bake the pancakes in a hot non-stick pan on both sides.

You can use a regular pan oiled with some coconut butter.

If you wish to keep the crepes soft, cover them with a lid.

Now we can prepare the topping.

Mash the banana and mix it with the tahini.

Spread the "cream" on top of the pancakes and garnish with fresh berries and some shredded coconut.

Of course, you can use any kind of topping you prefer.

Carob Pancakes

Ingredients:

2 **Eggs**
1 **Banana**
A pinch of **Salt**
A pinch of **Baking powder**
2 Tbsps. **Coconut butter** (melted)
3 1/2 Tbsps. **Water** (or coconut milk)
4 Tbsps. **Carob powder**

Instructions:

Start by beating the eggs in a large cup.

Mash the banana and add it to the eggs.

Next, add the salt, baking powder, the coconut butter and the water.

Blend the ingredients well with a whisk or a hand mixer.

Add the carob powder and continue to stir until the batter becomes fully homogenous.

The mixture may look a bit like a jelly, but do not worry – it is perfectly fine.

Bake the pancakes in a hot non-stick pan. Remember to spread the batter nicely on the pan because its consistency is not as liquid as the usual pancake mixtures.

GLUTEN-FREE
PIES AND CAKES

Fruit Pie

Ingredients:

For the bottom layer:
1 **Egg**
2 **Bananas**
2 Tbsps. **Carob powder**
2 Tbsps. **Apple powder**
1 Tbsp. **Coconut butter** (melted)
1 tsp. **Baking soda**
1/4 tsp. **Vanilla powder**

For the top layer:
2 **Apples**
1 **Peach**
3 Tbsps. **Yogurt**
3 Tbsps. **Coconut flour**
Some **Cinnamon** (optional)

Instructions:

First, we are going to prepare the bottom pie crust. Mix the ingredients well and blend them with a hand mixer or a blender.
Pour the mixture in a cake form (about 5"-6") and bake at 170° C/338° F for about 20 minutes (use the fan-assist option, if any). Take the half-baked crust out of the oven to rest until we make the icing.
Remove the seeds/pits from the fruits and cut them in medium chunks. Place them in a blender (or a kitchen

chopper) along with the yogurt and the coconut flour. Stir until the mixture becomes homogenous.

Pour the cream on top of the pie crust and resume baking the dish for 15-20 more minutes (until fully cooked).

Sprinkle some cinnamon on top, if you desire.

Apple Pie with Corn Meal

Ingredients:

4 cups **Apples** (preferably sour)
1 cup **Corn meal** (non-GMO)
1 cup **Gluten-free flour mix of choice**
2 tsps. **Baking powder** (gluten-free)
8 Tbsps. **Butter**
1 cup **Coconut sugar** (or other healthy sweetener of choice)
1 tsp. **Cinnamon**
1/2 cup **Walnuts**

Instructions:

Remove the seeds from the apples and grind the fruits in a kitchen chopper. Grind the walnuts as well – you do not need to turn them into powder.

Next, mix the apple puree with the cinnamon and the ground walnuts.

In another bowl, combine the dry ingredients – corn meal, the flour, baking powder and sugar.

Melt the butter.

Next, take a baking pan (about 8"/8") and cover it with baking paper.

Take 1/3 of the apple mix and spread it at the bottom of the pan. Cover it with 1/3 of the dry ingredient mix and pour some of the melted butter (about 2-3 Tbsps.).

Continue to interchange the layers until you finish with the last batch of dry flour mix at the top. Remember to pour some melted butter at the top as well.

Heat the oven at 180° C/ 356° F and bake for about 40 minutes until fully cooked.

Leave the pie to cool down and rest overnight.

My notes:

Easy Apple Pie

Ingredients:

3 **Apples** (sweet)
1 tsp. **Baking soda**
5 Tbsps. **Maple syrup** (or agave)
3 1/2 Tbsps. **Butter**
3 1/2 Tbsps. **Coconut butter**
1 1/2 cup **Gluten-free flour mix**
1 cup **Ground walnuts**
1 tsp. **Cinnamon**
A fistful of **Dry plums**

Instructions:

Take 2 of the apples, remove their seeds and grind them (or grate them). Dice the last apple in cubes.

Next, heat the two types of butter until they soften.

Cut the dry plums in small pieces.

Now we can prepare the batter.

Simply combine all ingredients and stir until they blend completely. You can use a hand mixer, if you wish.

In the meantime, heat the oven at 190° C/ 374° F.

Take a square cake mold and grease it with some coconut butter (or regular cow butter).

Pour the batter in and bake the pie for about 40 minutes until fully cooked.

Wait for the dessert to cool down completely before cutting it in pieces!

Enjoy!

Cinnamon Apple Pie

Ingredients:

1/2 cup **Melted butter** (or cow or coconut)
100 drops **Liquid stevia** (with 1:1 ratio to sugar)*
4 **Eggs**
1/2 cup **Almond flour**
3 Tbsps. **Coconut flour**
1 tsp. **Cinnamon**
1/2 tsp. **Baking soda**
1/2 tsp. **Salt**
1/2 cup **Walnuts** (ground)
2 cups **Fresh apples** (peeled and diced)

Instructions:

Mix the butter, stevia extract, the eggs, and blend them well.
Next, add the almond flour, the coconut flour, the cinnamon, baking soda, and the salt. Stir well to homogenize the mixture.
Consecutively, add the walnuts and the apple cubes and stir again.
Start heating the oven at 165° C/ 329° F.
Finally, pour the batter in an oiled baking pan (about 9" wide) and cook for 40-50 minutes until ready. Use a toothpick to check if the insides of the cake are well baked.
Take out of the oven and let it cool off completely.

*The quantity of the stevia will depend on the type of product you use. Most extracts have a ratio to sugar as follows:
1 cup sugar = 1 tsp. liquid or powdered stevia

1 Tbsp. sugar = 1/4 tsp. powdered (6-9 drops liquid stevia)
1 tsp. sugar = a pinch of powdered (2-4 drops liquid stevia)
Keep in mind that there are other types of stevia extracts with different ratios, for example 1:1.
Eventually, experiment and see which quantities suit your taste best!

Autumn Gluten-free Pie

Ingredients:

For the base:
2 **Egg yolks**
2 Tbsps. **Coconut butter** (melted)
4 Tbsps. **Date molasses**
1 tsp. **Baking powder**
1 tsp. **Vanilla extract**
1/2 cup **Rice flour**

For the cream:
1 cup **Boiled sweet chestnuts**
1/2 cup **Boiled pumpkin**
3 1/2 Tbsps. **Coconut milk**
10 **Dates** (pitted)
2 Tbsps. **Dark chocolate** (sugar-free)*

Instructions:

First, start by beating the egg yolks and mixing them with the coconut butter.

Blend the ingredients well, add the date syrup, the vanilla extract, and stir again.

In another large cup, mix the rice flour and the baking powder, and homogenize them completely.

Next, transfer the dry ingredients to the sweet mixture, and stir again with a fork (or a whisk).

Consecutively, start heating the oven at 170° C/338° F.

In the meantime, take a baking tray and cover it with baking paper.

Spread the pie batter in the container and bake for 15-20 minutes, or until fully cooked.

Next, take the pie crust out of the oven and let it cool down.

Meanwhile, we can prepare the cream.

Place the peeled and boiled chestnuts in a blender. Remove the skin from the pumpkin (if any) and add it in the kitchen appliance along with the coconut milk and the dates.

Blend everything nicely to form a homogenous cream.

Cover the pie with the sweet mixture and garnish with some dark chocolate chips on top.

*If you do not have sugar-free chocolate at your disposal, you can always make it on your own! You can find two of my favorite healthy chocolate recipes in my FREE ebook "12 Healthy Dessert Recipes"

Chestnut Pie

Ingredients:

For the base:
1 cup **Dates** (pitted)
1/2 cup **Sweet chestnuts** (boiled)
1/2 cup **Almond flour**
1/2 cup **Hazelnut flour**
1 cup **Coconut flour**
1/2 cup **Butter** (soft)
2 Tbsps. **Maple syrup**

For the cream:
1 cup **Ricotta cheese**
1 cup **Strained yogurt** (or high-fat Buffalo yogurt)
Some **Orange jam** – preferably homemade without white sugar (to taste)
Some **Cocoa powder** (to taste)
2 tsps. **Gelatin**
Some **Water** (enough to cover the gelatin)

Instructions:

The procedure is fairly easy!
Start by blending all the ingredients for the cake base in a kitchen robot (or a chopper).
When the mixture is ready, place it in your favorite cake ring mold and store in the fridge until it stiffens.
Meanwhile, prepare the cream.
Cover the gelatin with some cold water and wait for it to bulge up.

Next, place it in a double boiler, and warm it until it melts and becomes transparent.

Leave it aside to cool down a bit.

Next, blend all the other ingredients for the cream. If you wish, you can use a hand blender to homogenize the mixture more easily.

Now add the gelatin and stir again nicely to distribute it evenly.

Finally, pour the cream on top of the cake and bring it back to the fridge for a couple of hours.

That's it!

Here is how to make your own white sugar free orange jam!

My notes:

Homemade Orange Jam

Ingredients:

5 **Oranges** (bio)
1 **Lemon** (bio)
1 cup **Maple syrup** (or Muscovado sugar, coconut sugar, etc.)
Some **Water**

Instructions:

First, since we are going to use the zest from the citruses, it is best to use organic bio fruits not treated with toxic chemicals.

For extra protection, you can soak them in some apple cider vinegar water solution for 30 minutes beforehand. Just remember to rinse them thoroughly afterwards.

Now we can start making the jam!

Peel the oranges and cut the pulp in cubes.

Grate the lemon zest, peel off the white skin, and dice the pulp just like we did with the oranges.

Gently remove any seeds from the citruses.

Place the orange peels in a metal pot and cover them with some water.

Heat them on the stove on low temperature, and let them simmer for about 30 minutes.

Next, strain the orange zest, and mix it with half of the maple syrup, and the pulp from the citruses. Stir well and leave the mixture to soak overnight.

On the next day, heat the sweet mass on low temperature along with the remaining sweetener, and the grated lemon zest.

Let it cook until it starts to thicken to the desired consistency.

Remember to gently remove any foam from the top of the mixture with a slotted spoon.

When the citrus jam is ready, pour it in clean glass jars, and seal them tightly.

Turn them upside down and leave them to cool down to create vacuum.

Store in a dark and cool place!

Note: if you like this recipe, feel free to increase the quantities and make larger batches for the winter!

You can also adjust the quantity of the sweetener to match your taste and preferences!

My notes:

Lazy Balkan Pumpkin Burek (Tikvenik) I

Ingredients:

3 **Eggs**
1 Tbsp. **Cinnamon**
2 Tbsps. **Coconut flour**
1 Tbsp. **Coconut butter** (soft)
1 cup **Ground walnuts**
1-2 cups **Pumpkin**
1/2 cup **Raisins**
1/4 cup **Dry cranberries**
5-6 **Dates** (pitted)
Some **Water** (for the dry fruits)

Instructions:

Note: this recipe is very easy and it can be adjusted freely according to your taste and preferences. You can change the quantities of the walnuts, the pumpkin, and the fruits – if you want the dessert sweeter or not. It is totally up to you! I believe that in the kitchen, we can be our creative selves and experiment!

So, first, we soak the dry fruits in some water for 30-60 minutes until they soften.

In the meantime, grate the pumpkin, or mince it in the kitchen chopper.

When the fruits are ready, strain them and add them to the pumpkin.

Blend the ingredients as you continue to add the remaining components.

Start heating the oven to 180° C/ 356° F.

Place the mixture in a baking pan with the desired shape (preferably flat) and bake until fully cooked (about 45 minutes).

Lazy Balkan Pumpkin Burek (Tikvenik) II

Ingredients:

3/4 cup **Buckwheat flakes**
3/4 cup **Rice flakes**
4 Tbsps. **Yogurt**
6 Tbsps. **Coconut sugar**
1 1/2 tsp. **Baking powder**
1 tsp. **Ginger**
1 Tbsp. **Cinnamon**
3 1/2 Tbsps. **Butter** (melted)
1 1/2 Tbsp. **Olive oil**
2 cups **Pumpkin** (boiled or steamed)
2 cups **Walnuts** (ground)
A few chunks **Butter** (hard) - optional

Instructions:

First, we will start by mixing the dry ingredients.
Combine the buckwheat flakes, the rice flakes, coconut sugar, ginger powder, cinnamon, and the baking powder.
Stir to blend them well.
Next, add the yogurt and continue to stir the mixture.

Consecutively, add the melted butter, the olive oil, the soft pumpkin, and blend once again. Feel free to use a hand mixer or a blender to make the process easier.

At this point, you can start heating the oven to 180° C/ 356° F.

Finally, add the walnuts and stir the batter with a spoon.

Take a baking pan (preferably flat) and cover it with baking paper.

Pour the mixture in and place several chunks of butter at the top, if you wish to make the burek softer.

Bake in the preheated oven until fully cooked!

Gluten-free Pie with Pears

Ingredients:

5 **Pears**
4 1/2 Tbsps. **Butter**
2 Tbsps. **Maple syrup**
3 Tbsps. **Muscovado sugar**
1 tsp. **Vanilla extract**
1 cup **Cottage cheese** (curd)
4 Tbsps. **Corn flour**
3 1/2 Tbsps. **Ground walnuts**
1 Tbsp. **Gluten-free flour mix of choice** (optional)
1/2 tsp. **Ginger powder**
1 **Egg**
1/4 tsp. **Salt**
1 tsp. **Cinnamon**

Instructions:

First, wash the pears, remove any seeds and handles, and cut them in thin slices.

Next, we can prepare the caramel. Take a non-stick frying pan or a saucepan, and place 1 Tbsp. Muscovado sugar, the maple syrup and 2 Tbsps. butter.

Heat them and stir until they blend completely and form a nice golden caramel mixture.

Next, take the pan off the heat and place the pear slices and the ground walnuts in the caramel sauce.

Now we can start preparing the crust.

Mix the cottage cheese with the corn flour in a large bowl.

Add the remaining sugar (2 Tbsps.) and blend them well.

Consecutively, add the ginger power, the cinnamon, the egg, and stir well to homogenize the dough.

Add the remaining butter (2 1/2 Tbsps.) and continue to blend the mixture. If it becomes too sticky, add 1 Tbsp. gluten-free flour.

Next, take a baking tray and cover it with baking paper. Spread the cake dough on top and bake in a preheated oven (at 175° C/ 347° F) for 20 minutes.

Finally, pour the caramel sauce with the pears on top of the pie crust and continue baking until fully cooked. The edges of the pie crust will become nicely golden and crispy.

Healthy Cocoa Cake with Bananas

Ingredients:

5 **Eggs**
2 **Bananas**
4 Tbsps. **Curd** (cottage cheese)
3-4 Tbsps. **Cocoa powder**
2 tsps. **Cinnamon**
A pinch of **Nutmeg**
1 tsp. **Vanilla powder**
1/2 tsp. **Baking powder** (gluten-free)

Instructions:

Simply blend the ingredients well with a hand mixer.
Pour the mixture in a non-stick baking pan and bake in a preheated oven (at 180° C/ 356° F) for about 25 minutes. Use a tooth pick to check if the cake is fully cooked.
Bon Appetite!

My notes:

Banana Cake

Ingredients:

4 **Eggs**
3 **Bananas**
10 **Dates** (pitted)
1/2 cup **Ground walnuts**
2 tsps. **Baking powder**
2 Tbsps. **Sesame tahini**
1 Tbsp. **Maple syrup** (or agave)
1-2 Tbsps. **Cocoa powder**
1/4 tsp. **Vanilla extract**
1/2 tsp. **Cinnamon**
1/2 cup **Olive or sunflower oil**

Instructions:

Peel and cut the bananas in large chunks.

Place all ingredients in a kitchen robot and blend them well.

Take a cake form or a baking pan, and grease it with some oil.

Pour the cake mixture in and bake at 200° C/ 392° F for about 25-30 minutes. Use a toothpick or a wooden stick to check if the cake is ready.

Take out of the oven and let it cool down completely before cutting and serving it.

Juicy Carrot Cake with Apples

Ingredients:

4 **Eggs**
1/2 cup **Raw almonds**
1 cup **Carrots**
2 **Apples**
8 Tbsps. **Yogurt**
4-5 Tbsps. **Coconut flour**
1 tsp. **Baking soda**
1 tsp. **Apple cider vinegar** (ACV)
2-3 tsps. **Coconut butter**
3-4 Tbsps. **Maple syrup**
Some **Honey** (to taste)
1 Tbsp. **Ghee** (or regular butter)

Instructions:

Note: if you like making carrot juices, you can use the remaining pulp for this recipe! Alternatively, simply grate or mince the carrots in a kitchen robot.

Now let's mince the almonds in the kitchen chopper as well.

Next, beat the eggs and mix them with the ground nuts.

Cut one apple in half and grate one of the parts. Add it to the shredded carrots and mix well.

Transfer the veggies and fruit mixture to the eggs and almonds, and stir.

Next, add the yogurt, the coconut flour, and the maple syrup. Feel free to adjust the quantity of the sweetener to match your preferences!

Consecutively, add the baking soda, the ACV, and blend well.

At this point, you should have reached the consistency of cake batter. If not, add more coconut flour.

Now you can start heating the oven at 180° C/ 356° F. Bake the cake for about 40 minutes until fully cooked. Note that the cake can be a bit moist, especially if you are using whole carrots instead of pulp from a juice. But do not worry – this is the goal here – to make a juicy mouthwatering dessert.

In the meantime, we can prepare the cream.

Take the remaining one and a half apple, remove any seeds and stems, and heat the fruit in a pot with some water. Leave it to simmer until it becomes nice and soft.

Next, mash the fruit with a fork, and add some ghee and honey to taste.

When the cake is ready, take it out of the oven and leave it cool down.

Finally, spread the cream on top and enjoy!

My notes:

Orange Cake with Dates

Ingredients:

1 1/2 cup **Dates** (pitted)
2 **Oranges**
1/2 cup **Butter** (soft)
2 **Eggs**
1 tsp. **Baking powder**
1/2 cup **Gluten-free flour mix of choice**
A pinch of **Salt**

Instructions:

First, cut the dates in halves.

Next, squeeze the juice from the oranges and mix it with the baking powder.

After that, add the dates and homogenize the mixture with a blender or a kitchen chopper.

In another container, beat the eggs and blend them with the butter.

Slowly add the flour while stirring continuously.

Next, add the date and orange puree and stir to blend the dough completely.

Transfer the mixture to a suitable cake or a bread mold and bake in a preheated oven (to 180° C/ 356° F) until fully cooked. Check with a toothpick if the dessert is ready.

Autumn Cake with Pears and Almonds

Ingredients:

3 **Eggs**
2-3 Tbsps. **Maple syrup** (or agave)
1 1/2 cup **Pears**
1 cup **Ground almonds**
2-3 Tbsps. **Butter**
1 tsp. **Baking powder**
1 tsp. **Cinnamon**
1/2 tsp. **Baking soda**
A pinch of **Salt**

Instructions:

First, peel the pears and remove their seeds. Grate the fruits nicely or puree them.

Next, separate the egg whites from the egg yolks.

Whisk the egg yolks in a large bowl and add the remaining ingredients (except the egg whites).

Beat the egg whites until stiff and add them to the cake mix.

Pour the batter in a greased cake form or a baking pan. Bake the cake in a preheated oven at 160° C/ 320° F for about 50 minutes until fully cooked.

Enjoy!

Sugar-free Cake with Dry Apricots

Ingredients:

For the cake base:
6 **Eggs**
15 **Dates** (pitted)
3 Tbsps. **Cocoa powder**

For the icing:
1/2 cup **Dry apricots** (not treated with sugar)
1/2 Tbsp. **Cocoa powder**
2-3 **Dates** (pitted)
Some **Pure water** (for soaking the apricots)

Instructions:

First, we need to soak the dry fruits for at least 4 hours. It is best to leave them overnight to become juicier.

The next day, strain the apricots, but do not throw away the water – we will need it later on in the recipe!

Next, separate the egg yolks from the whites.

Place the egg yolks in a kitchen robot, add the pitted dates (15) and mince them well. Stir until the mixture is fully homogenous and foamy. Now add the cocoa powder (3 Tbsps.) and stir again to blend the ingredients well.

Next, in another container whisk the egg whites until stiff. Use a hand mixer, if you wish to make the process easier.

Consecutively, combine the egg whites with the cocoa mixture and gently blend with a spoon or a spatula.

Now it is time to heat the oven at 160° C/ 320° F and bake the cake for about 15 minutes. You can use the fan-assist function, if you have one.

When the base of the cake is fully cooked, take it out of the oven and leave it to cool down completely.

Next, we can start preparing the icing.

Place the soaked apricots, the dates, and some of the fruit water (about 4 1/2 Tbsps.) in a blender and puree them. The goal is to reach a nice homogenous creamy consistency.

Cover the cake with the cream and the dessert is ready for consumption!

Easy Strawberry Cake with Mascarpone

Ingredients:

For the cake base:
1 cup **Almond flour**
1-2 Tbsps. **Coconut butter** (melted)
9-14 **Dates** (pitted)

For the icing:
2 cups **Mascarpone**
2 Tbsps. **Honey**
1 Tbsp. **Sour cream**
Some **Strawberries** (for decoration)

Instructions:

Blend the ingredients for the cake base in a blender or a kitchen chopper.

When the mixture becomes homogenous, transfer it to a suitable cake form (the adjustable cake ring is best).

Next, place the cake in the fridge for a couple of hours to harden.

Now we can prepare the icing.

Mix all the ingredients and blend them completely.

Spread the cream on the cake base and even it with a spatula (or a knife).

Decorate with the fruits and bring the cake back in the fridge until consumption!

Lemon Cake with Mascarpone

Ingredients:

For the cake layers:
4 **Eggs**
1 1/2 cup **Yogurt**
1/2 tsp. **Baking soda**
1 cup **Rice flour**
A pinch of **Salt**
1 tsp. **Vanilla extract**
Some **Coconut butter**

For the icing:
1 cup **Mascarpone**
1 cup **Sour cream**
1 Tbsp. **Honey**
1 Tbsp. **Lemon cream** (recipe below)

Instructions:

First, we will prepare the cake layers. The technology is similar to making simple pancakes.

Beat the eggs with a whisk.

Next, mix the yogurt with the baking soda and let it froth for a bit.

Add the yogurt to the eggs along with the rice flour, salt, and the vanilla extract.

Continue to whisk the mixture until you reach a homogenous mass. Note: do not use a hand mixer for this recipe!

Next, take a pan with a lid and oil it with some coconut butter.

Bake the pancakes for a few minutes with the lid on. Butter each layer after you flip it.

The mixture will yield about 6 sponge pancakes. Remember to leave the layers to cool down completely before spreading the cream and assembling the cake!

In the meantime, we can make the cream.

Simply mix the ingredients and blend them completely.

When the pancakes' temperature drops down, start stacking them and spreading some cream between each layer.

Cover the cake with the remaining icing and voila!

Store in the fridge to keep its form and prevent the cream from melting!

Gluten-free Cake with Lemon Cream

Ingredients:

4 **Eggs**
3 tsps. **Lemon cream** (recipe below)
1/2 cup **Maple syrup** (adjust to taste, if you need to)
2 Tbsps. **Sesame tahini**
2/3 cup **Almond milk**
2/3 cup **Almond pulp** (left from the almond milk)
1/2 tsp. **Baking soda**
2 1/2 Tbsps. **Butter** (melted)
1 cup **Sour cream**
3 Tbsps. **Apple flour**
5 Tbsps. **Ground almonds**
1 Tbsp. **Carob powder**
Some **Desiccated coconut** (optional)

Instructions:

This cake is very easy and fast to prepare, so you can start by heating the oven at 180° C/ 356° F right away!

Next, simply place all ingredients (except the desiccated coconut) in a blender (or a kitchen robot) and mince until you reach a nice homogenous cake mixture.

Pour the batter in a suitable mold and bake in the pre-heated oven for about 35 minutes or until fully cooked.

Take the cake out of the furnace and cover it with some coconut shreds, if you desire.

Cut the dessert after it has cooled down completely.

Lemon Cream

Ingredients:

1/2 cup **Butter**
3 **Lemons** (bio)
3 **Eggs**
1 cup **Maple syrup** (or Muscovado sugar, coconut sugar, etc.)

Instructions:

First, melt the butter in a metal pot on low temperature.

Next, wash the lemons, grate their zest, and squeeze out the juice.

Consecutively, beat the eggs in a large bowl and blend them with the maple syrup (or sugar). Add the lemon zest, the juice, and the melted butter.

Stir again to homogenize the mixture.

Transfer the cream in a metal pot and heat it on low temperature.

Let the mixture simmer for 3 minutes, but don't forget to stir it throughout the entire time.

If you wish to consume the cream right away, simply leave it to cool down.

If you want to preserve it for longer, pour it in a glass jar while it is still hot, seal it tightly, and turn it upside down to create vacuum.

Raspberry Jelly Cake

Ingredients:

For the cake base:
1/2 cup **Raw cashew**
1/2 cup **Raw sunflower seeds** (peeled)
2 Tbsps. **Coconut butter** (melted)
2-3 Tbsps. **Flax seed powder**
12-15 **Dates** (pitted)

For the jelly:
2 cups **Raspberries**
1 cup **Water**
1 1/2 Tbsp. **Gelatin**
Some **Water**
1-2 Tbsps. **Honey**
Some more **Raspberries** (for decoration)

Instructions:

First, we can prepare the jelly, because it will consume quite some time.
Mix the raspberries with the water in a metal pot and heat them.
Stir well to blend them as much as possible.
In the meantime, mix the gelatin with some water and wait for it to bulge up.
Next, heat it in a double boiler until it becomes transparent.
Now mix the gelatin with the hot raspberries and stir well.
Take the mixture off the heat and let it cool down to body temperature.

EASY GLUTEN FREE DESSERTS • 59

Next, add the honey and stir again nicely.

Consecutively, we can start making the cake itself.

Blend all ingredients in a kitchen chopper or a robot until fully homogenous.

Transfer the mixture in an adjustable cake ring mold. Press gently to form the base of the cake.

Next, pour the liquid jelly on top of the base layer.

Garnish with some raspberries, and bring the cake in the fridge for several hours to harden.

Zucchini (yup!) Cake

Ingredients:

3 **Eggs**
1/2 cup **Maple syrup** (adjust to taste, if needed)
1 cup **Gluten-free flour mix**
1 cup **Zucchini**
2 **Carrots**
1 **Apple**
1 tsp. **Cinnamon**
A pinch of **Ground cloves**
A pinch of **Nutmeg**
1 tsp. **Vanilla extract**
1/2 tsp. **Baking soda**
1 tsp. **Baking powder**
3 Tbsps. **Yogurt**
1 tsp. **Apple cider vinegar** (ACV)
1/2 cup **Coconut butter** (melted)
1/2 cup **Ground walnuts**

Instructions:

First, peel and grind the zucchini. Squeeze any juice from it as much as you can.

Next, grind the carrots as well; remove the seeds from the apple, and cut it in small pieces.

Now we can prepare the batter for the cake.

Mix the baking soda with the yogurt and let it froth.

In the meantime, beat the eggs, and mix them with the maple syrup.

Start adding all the remaining ingredients for the cake – the flour, ground zucchini, carrots, apple cubes, the spices, the yogurt with the baking soda, baking powder, ACV, coconut butter, and the walnuts.

Stir well to blend the mixture. Use a hand mixer, if you wish to make the process easier.

Next, heat the oven at 180° C/ 356° F. Pour the batter in a flat baking tray covered with baking paper.

Finally, bake the cake for about 30 minutes until fully cooked.

My notes:

Fake Lava Cake

Ingredients:

2 Tbsps. **Flax seed flour**
1 cup **Rice flour**
4-5 Tbsps. **Carob powder**
4 **Eggs**
1/3 cup **Muscovado sugar**
2/3 cup **Coconut sugar**
1/2 cup **Soft butter** (or melted)

Instructions:

First, we mix the dry ingredients – the flax seeds, the rice flour, and the carob powder. Blend them well.

Next, beat the eggs and add the two types of sugar. Whisk the mixture until it becomes nice and fluffy.

After that, add the butter and continue to blend the ingredients.

Consecutively, add the flour mixture and stir until the batter becomes fully homogenous.

Heat the oven at 180° C/ 356° F and bake the cake for 6-7 minutes. Next, open the oven door and continue baking for 5-6 more minutes.

The insides of the cake will remain nice and soft with the lava-like effect.

Bon appetite!

Fast and Easy Cake

Ingredients:

4 **Eggs**
3 **Bananas**
2 Tbsps. **Coconut butter**
1 cup **Yogurt**
1 tsp. **Baking soda**
1 cup **Coconut flour**
3 Tbsps. **Coconut sugar**
1 Tbsp. **Carob powder**
A fistful of **Walnuts**

Instructions:

First, beat the eggs and mash the bananas.

Mix the yogurt with the baking soda and let it dissolve completely and froth.

Next, melt the coconut butter in a double boiler, if it is hard.

Combine the eggs with the banana puree, coconut butter, the yogurt, and stir well.

In another container, mix the flour, coconut sugar, carob powder, and blend them well.

Add the dry ingredients to the main mixture and stir again until the batter becomes fully homogenous.

Grind the walnuts in small chunks and add them to the cake mixture.

Heat the oven to 180° C/ 356° F and bake the cake until fully cooked. The time will depend on the cake mold you use and your particular oven. (You know each oven has its own character and behavior!)

Peach Cake

Ingredients:

3 **Eggs**

2 tsps. **Carob powder**

2 tsps. **Coconut flour**

1/2 cup **Cream cheese**

1 tsp. **Vanilla extract**

2 Tbsps. **Hazelnut tahini**

3 **Peaches** (fully ripe and sweet)

Some **Coconut butter** (melted)

Instructions:

The recipe is extremely easy!

Simply blend all ingredients (except the peaches) with a hand mixer or a blender.

Transfer the batter in a baking tray covered with baking paper and greased with some coconut butter.

Heat the oven at 180° C/ 356° F.

In the meantime, cut the peaches in slices and place them on top of the cake mixture.

Bake the dessert for about 25 minutes or until fully cooked.

My notes:

Raspberry Dessert (Cake)

Ingredients:

4 **Eggs**
1/4 - 1/2 cup **Coconut sugar**
1 tsp. **Salt**
2 Tbsps. **Butter** (melted)
1 cup **Almond milk**
1/2 cup **Gluten-free flour mix** (self-rising)
1-2 tsps. **Vanilla extract**
Some **Raspberries** (enough to cover the cake mold)

Instructions:

Take a round cake pan (about 9"x3") and cover it with baking paper. If you do not have such mold, use whatever baking pan you have with similar dimensions and volume.

Arrange the fruits at the bottom of the pan, and start heating the oven to 180° C/ 356° F.

Next, we can start with the cake mix. This dessert is a bit different from the usual cakes because its batter is more liquid (like the ones for pancakes). So, do not worry!

Simply blend the ingredients in a kitchen chopper, a robot, or a blender until you reach a homogenous mass.

Pour the batter on top of the raspberries and bake the cake for about 45 minutes (or until fully cooked). You know, different ovens do not behave equally! ☺

Bon appetite!

Blueberry Cake

Ingredients:

For the base:
3 **Eggs**
5 Tbsps. **Dry blueberries** (without sugar)
Some **Orange juice** (freshly squeezed)
8 **Dates** (pitted)
1 Tbsp. **Coconut butter** (soft)
1/2 cup **Yogurt**
1 tsp. **Baking soda**
2 Tbsps. **Carob powder**
2 Tbsps. **Coconut flour**
1-2 tsps. **Vanilla extract**

For the icing:
1 cup **Strained yogurt** (or high-fat Buffalo yogurt)
2-3 **Average tangerines**

Instructions:

First, cover the blueberries in some orange juice until they soften.

At this point you can start heating the oven to 200° C/ 392° F.

Mix the yogurt and the baking soda, and leave the mixture to froth for a bit.

Next, blend the eggs, the vanilla extract, coconut butter, and the dates in a kitchen robot.

Now we can add the bubbly yogurt to the mixture and blend again.

Add the coconut flour and the carob powder, and stir until you homogenize the batter.

Take a suitable flat baking tray and cover it with baking paper. Pour the cake mixture in and bake until the base is fully cooked (the toothpick comes out clean).

Next, take the dessert out of the oven and leave it to cool down completely.

In the meantime, blend the yogurt and the peeled tangerines in a kitchen chopper or a robot. Be careful not to let any seeds from the citrus fruit to end up in the icing!

Cover the cake with the frosting and place it in the fridge. If you wish, you can adjust the quantities of the icing depending on your preferences.

Almond Pulp Cake

Ingredients:

3 **Eggs**
1 cup **Yogurt**
1/2 tsp. **Baking soda**
8 **Dates** (pitted)
2 **Large dry figs**
1 tsp. **Vanilla extract**
A pinch of **Ginger powder**
1 tsp. **Cinnamon**
1/2 cup **Almond pulp**
1 **Apple**
2 Tbsps. **Rice flour**
1 Tbsp. **Coconut butter** (melted)

Instructions:

This is an excellent way to utilize the remaining pulp from preparing your own almond milk (or any other type of nut milk)!

First, beat the eggs in a large bowl.

In another cup, mix the yogurt with the baking soda and stir.

While the soda starts to react in the yogurt, cut the apple in pieces and remove any seeds.

Mince the fruit in a kitchen chopper until you reach a nice apple puree.

Next, add the dates and the figs and continue stirring until they blend nicely.

Now we can prepare the batter – simply combine all ingredients and stir with a hand mixer until you reach a homogenous consistency.

Pour the mixture in a suitable cake form and heat the oven at 170° C/338° F.

Bake the dessert for about 40 minutes until fully cooked.

My notes:

Marble Cake with Soda

Ingredients:

5 **Eggs**
2 tsps. **Liquid stevia***
1 cup **Soda** (carbonated water)
3/4 cup **Coconut butter** (or other type of healthy oil of choice)
3 1/2 cups **Gluten-free flour mix**
2 tsps. **Baking powder**
2 Tbsps. **Cocoa powder**

Instructions:

First, beat the eggs in a large bowl along with the stevia, melted coconut butter, and the soda.

In another cup, mix the flour with the baking powder and blend them well.

Combine the flour with the egg mixture and stir again to homogenize the batter.

Take a suitable cake form and pour 3/4 of the mixture in.

Next, mix the remaining batter with the cocoa powder and blend again.

Gently pour the brown mass into the cake form and we are ready for the final part.

Heat the oven at 180° C/ 356° F and bake the dessert for about 40-45 minutes until fully cooked!

*The quantity of the stevia will depend on the type of product you use. Most extracts have a ratio to sugar as follows:
1 cup sugar = 1 tsp. liquid or powdered stevia

1 Tbsp. sugar = 1/4 tsp. powdered (6-9 drops liquid stevia)
1 tsp. sugar = a pinch of powdered (2-4 drops liquid stevia)
Keep in mind that there are other types of stevia extracts with different ratios, for example 1:1.
Eventually, experiment and see what quantities suit your taste best!

Simple Gluten-free Cake

Ingredients:

4 **Eggs**
1 cup **Coconut sugar** (adjust to taste, if you need to)
2 tsps. **Ghee**
2 Tbsps. **Sesame tahini**
1 cup **Coconut milk**
2 tsps. **Baking powder**
8 Tbsps. **Gluten-free flour mix**
2 Tbsps. **Maple syrup**
6 **Strawberries**
A handful of **Desiccated coconut** (for decoration)

Instructions:

First, beat the eggs in a large container.
Add the coconut sugar, the ghee (soft), tahini, and the coconut milk.
Blend the ingredients well.
In another cup, mix the flour with the baking powder, and stir well.
Transfer the dry mixture to the batter, and blend again.
Cut the strawberries in pieces and add them to the cake mix.

If you wish to consume them fresh and take advantage of all of their nutrients, leave them for the final part.

Pour the batter in a cake form and bake at 180° C/ 356° F until fully cooked. In this case, you do not need to preheat the oven.

When the dessert is ready and cooled down completely, turn it upside down, cover it with the maple syrup, the desiccated coconut, and the strawberries.

Enjoy!

Flour-less Orange Cake

Ingredients:

For the cake:
4 **Eggs**
2 **Oranges** (bio)
1 cup **Raw nuts** (walnuts, hazelnuts, almonds, etc.)
1 cup **Coconut pulp** (or desiccated coconut)
5 Tbsps. **Baking soda** (salt or apple cider vinegar)
Some **Clean filtered water**

For the cream:
1/2 cup **Dark chocolate** (preferably sugar-free)*
1 cup **Cooking cream**

Instructions:

First, we need to soak the oranges to remove any bugs and harmful microorganisms. We perform this step because we will use the whole fruits with their zest.

There are a couple of ways this can be done. One option is to mix the baking soda with some clean water and soak the oranges in the solution for at least 30 minutes.

Alternatively, you can use salt or apple cider vinegar to prepare the cleansing liquid.

Next, rinse the fruits thoroughly with water and boil them for about half an hour until they soften.

In the meantime, you can grind the nuts in a kitchen chopper, if not done already.

Next, place the boiled citrus fruits in a blender and mince them nicely.

Now add the eggs, the ground nuts, the coconut pulp, and a little bit of baking soda (1/2 -1 tsp.).

Continue to stir with the blender until the mixture becomes fully homogenous.

Now we can start heating the oven at 200° C/ 392° F and bake the cake for about 20 minutes.

Meanwhile, we can prepare the cream.

Simply melt the chocolate in a double boiler, and add the cream.

Stir until the mixture blends completely, and take it off the heat.

When the cake is ready and out of the oven, cover it with the icing, and enjoy!

*If you do not have sugar-free chocolate at your disposal, you can always make it on your own! You can find two of my favorite healthy chocolate recipes in my FREE ebook "12 Healthy Dessert Recipes"

Gluten-free Orange Cake

Ingredients:

2 **Eggs**
1 cup **Yogurt**
4 Tbsps. **Maple syrup** (or agave)
2 Tbsps. **Coconut butter** (melted)
1 tsp. **Baking powder**
2-3 Tbsps. **Gluten-free oat flour**
1 Tbsp. **Flaxseed flour**
1 Tbsp. **Cocoa powder**
1 tsp. **Vanilla extract**
1 **Orange** (bio)
Some **Gluten-free oatmeal**
5 Tbsps. **Baking soda** (salt or apple cider vinegar)
Some **Clean filtered water**

Instructions:

Since we will be using the whole orange in this recipe, it is best to perform the same cleansing procedure like the previous citrus cake.
Mix the baking soda with the filtered water and soak the orange for half an hour in it.

In the meantime, we can start preparing the cake itself.

Beat the eggs in a large bowl.

Next, add the yogurt, maple syrup, coconut butter, the vanilla extract, and blend well.

Rinse the orange thoroughly and peel off its skin. Grind the zest and squeeze the juice from the fruit.

Add the orange liquid to the sweet egg mixture, and stir again.

In another container, mix the dry ingredients – oat flour, baking powder, flaxseed flour, cocoa powder, the orange zest, and several tablespoons of the oatmeal.

Now combine the dry and the liquid ingredients to prepare the cake batter.

Blend completely, and add more oatmeal, if you need to make the consistency thicker.

Finally, heat the oven at 170° C/338° F and bake the cake until fully cooked. Remember to check if the cake is ready with a wooden toothpick!

My notes:

Gluten-free Cake with Figs

Ingredients:

For the base:
1/3 cup **Yogurt**
1/2 tsp. **Baking powder**
3 Tbsps. **Coconut butter** (melted)
5 Tbsps. **Rice flour**
1 tsp. **Carob powder**

For the icing:
2 Tbsps. **Strained yogurt** (or Buffalo yogurt)
1 **Large fig** (firm and not too ripe)

Instructions:

The preparation of this recipe is very easy!
Start heating the oven to 180° C/ 356° F.
Next, mix the yogurt with the baking soda and let it froth for a bit.
Add the coconut butter, the rice flour, the carob powder, and blend well with a hand mixer or a blender.
Take a flat baking pan and cover it with baking paper.
Pour the mixture in and bake for about 20 minutes in the pre-heated oven.
In the meantime, cut the fig in thin slices. Add more figs, if needed.
When the cake is fully cooked and cooled down, cover it with the strained yogurt and arrange the fig slices on top.
Store the dessert in the fridge to maintain its shape.

Marble Cake on a Budget

Ingredients:

3 **Eggs**
A pinch of **Salt**
1/2 cup **Muscovado sugar** (or other healthy alternative)
3 1/2 Tbsps. **Butter** (melted)
1 cup **Kefir**
1 tsp. **Baking soda**
1 tsp. **Vanilla extract**
1 cup **Buckwheat flour**
1 tsp. **Baking powder**
1 Tbsp. **Cocoa powder**
1 Tbsp. **Water**

Instructions:

First, mix the kefir with the baking soda and stir. Leave the mixture to froth.
In the meantime, beat the eggs in a large bowl.
Add the sugar, butter, vanilla extract, the salt, and blend nicely.
Next, add the kefir, the buckwheat flour, baking powder, and stir again.
Use a hand mixer or a blender to homogenize the mixture completely.
At this point, you can start heating the oven at 150° C/ 302° F.
Pour about 3/4 of the batter in a cake form.

Next, mix the remaining mixture with the cocoa powder and the water. Blend the ingredients completely, and pour the dark mass into the cake form.

Finally, bake the dessert until fully cooked. The time will depend on your particular oven and the cake mold you use. Check with a toothpick to see if the cake is ready.

Marble Cake with Ricotta Cheese

Ingredients:

For the dark part:
3/4 cup **Butter** (soft)
1 cup **Muscovado sugar** (or coconut sugar)
2 **Eggs**
1/2 cup **Gluten-free flour mix of choice**
3 1/2 Tbsps. **Cocoa powder**

For the white part:
1 cup **Ricotta cheese** (or cottage cheese)
3 1/2 Tbsps. **Muscovado sugar** (or coconut sugar)
1 tsp. **Baking powder**
1 **Egg**

Instructions:

First, we need to grind all the sugar and turn it into powder. Simply take a coffee grinder or a kitchen chopper and grind the sweetener.

Next, mix 1 cup of the powdered sugar with the soft butter and blend them well until you reach a nice fluffy mixture.

Now add the eggs one by one as you are still stirring the batter.

Next, add the flour and the cocoa powder and blend the mixture once again. Be careful not to leave any dry lumps in the batter!

At this point, you can start heating the oven to the usual 180° C/ 356° F.

After that, take a rectangular cake mold (or whatever shape you have) and cover it with baking paper.

Now we can continue with the white part of the batter.

Mix the ricotta cheese with the remaining powdered sugar and blend them with a whisk.

Add the egg and stir again.

We can start arranging the marble cake.

Pour half of the cocoa batter in the baking pan and trim it nicely.

Next, pour the ricotta mixture, and finally – the remaining of the brown mass.

Take a suitable utensil (like a spatula or a knife) and gently move through the batter to make any interesting marble patterns.

Bake the dessert for about 45 minutes (or until fully cooked).

Remember to leave the cake to cool down completely before cutting it in pieces!

Bon appetite!

Gluten-free Cake for Special Occasions

Ingredients:

For the base:
6 **Eggs**
1/2 cup **Dates** (pitted)
3 Tbsps. **Coconut butter** (melted)
2 tsps. **Vanilla extract**
1 cup **Yogurt**
1/2 tsp. **Baking soda**
4 Tbsps. **Rice flour**
1 tsp. **Baking powder**
4 Tbsps. **Coconut flour**
4 tsps. **Carob powder**
5 tsps. **Gluten-free flour mix of choice**
1/2 cup **Dry cranberries** (sugar-free)
12 **Dry apricots** (sugar-free)
1 **Orange**
Some **Water** (to cover the apricots)

For the icing:
3 1/2 cups **Strained yogurt**
1 cup **Sour cream**
4 Tbsps. **Agave syrup**
2 Tbsps. **Coconut butter** (melted)

For the decoration:
2 Tbsps. **Cocoa butter** (melted)
1 tsp. **Carob powder**
2 tsps. **Hazelnut tahini**

Instructions:

First, squeeze the juice from the orange and soak the cranberries in it for about 15 minutes.

Cover the apricots with some water and leave them to soak as well for 30 minutes.

Next, mix the yogurt with the baking soda and let it froth for a bit.

Meanwhile, blend the eggs with the dates, coconut butter, and the vanilla extract.

Add the bubbly yogurt and stir again.

Next, add all the dry ingredients – rice flour, carob powder, coconut flour, gluten-free flour mix, the baking powder, and blend again thoroughly to reach a homogeneous mass.

Now strain the fruits and cut the apricots in small pieces.

Add them to the cake mix, and you can start heating the oven to 170° C/338° F.

Take a cake form (it could be 10"x3"), pour the mixture in, and bake for about 25 minutes. Use the fan-assist function, if you have it.

In the meantime, we can prepare the icing.

Mix the yogurt with the sour cream and blend them nicely with a whisk.

Next, add the agave syrup, the butter, and continue to whisk until the cream is fully blended.

The preparation of the frosting is very easy as well – simply mix the ingredients in a cup and stir until they blend completely.

When the cake is fully cooked and cooled down, cover it thoroughly with the white cream (cover everything – the top and the sides).

Garnish with the carob cream on top with the desired shapes.

Gluten-free Garash Cake

Ingredients:

8 **Eggs** (fresh, organic, and sanitized)
1 1/2 cup **Coconut sugar**
1 cup **Butter**
5 Tbsps. **Cocoa powder**
1 cup **Milk**
3 cups **Ground walnuts**
1 Tbsp. **Rum** (or orange juice)
1 tsp. **Vanilla extract**

Instructions:

First, we need to turn the coconut sugar into powder. Grind the sweetener in a coffee grinder or a chopper.

Next, separate the egg yolks from the whites.

Now we will prepare 3 different mixtures as follows:

Mixture #1: mix half of the powdered sugar with the egg yolks, and blend them well with a hand mixer (or a blender).

Mixture #2: mix the remaining sugar with the egg whites, and whisk until stiff, you can use a suitable kitchen tool as well to make the process easier – hand mixer, a blender, or a whisk.

Consecutively, add the ground walnuts to the white fluffy mixture, and gently stir with a spoon or a spatula to preserve the volume of the mixture.

Mixture #3: take the butter, and mix it with the milk and the cocoa powder. Heat the mass on low temperature, and let it simmer until it thickens a little bit. Remember to stir to avoid the milk from burning as much as possible.

Next, take it off the heat and let it cool down a bit. After that, add the rum extract (or the orange juice) and blend them well.

Now it gets interesting!

Combine mixture #1 and #3.

Consecutively, divide this mass into 4 equal parts.

Take 3 parts of the whole (3/4) and blend it with mixture #2.

Now you can start heating the oven to 180° C/ 356° F.

Take a suitable baking pan and cover it with some butter. Pour the batter in and bake for 20-30 minutes until fully cooked.

Next, wait for the cake to cool down completely and pour that reaming part (1/4) of mixture on top.

Place the dessert in the fridge to harden for several hours.

If you desire, you can decorate the cake with whatever you prefer – nuts, desiccated coconut, fruits, etc.

My notes:

Mini Pancake Cake

Ingredients:

For the pancakes:
1 cup **Rice flour**
1 cup **Coconut milk**
1 **Egg**
1 Tbsp. **Agave syrup**
2 Tbsps. **Olive oil**
2 tsps. **Baking powder**

For the cream:
2 **Bananas**
Some **Strained yogurt** (or high-fat buffalo yogurt)

Instructions:

Blend all ingredients for the pancakes. Adjust the quantities of the flour and milk, if you need to reach the desired constancy of thick liquid.

Bake the pancakes as usual and leave them to cool down. Remember not to keep them stacked or they will become too moist from the condensed water.

Next, we can prepare the cream. Simply blend the ingredients in a kitchen chopper or a robot. Add more yogurt or bananas to reach the desired sweetness.

Start assembling the cake by spreading some of the cream between the pancakes. Remember to leave some of the mixture to cover the cake as well!

Carob Mini Cake with Walnuts

Ingredients:

3 **Eggs**
1/2 cup **Coconut butter** (melted)
1 cup **Gluten-free flour mix**
2 Tbsps. **Carob powder**
3-4 Tbsps. **Maple syrup** (or other healthy sweetener of choice)
A fistful of **Walnuts**
A fistful of **Dates** (pitted)

Instructions:

Beat the eggs in a bowl and add the coconut butter, the carob powder, the flour and the maple syrup. Note: you can experiment and change the quantity of the sweetener to match your taste.

Blend the ingredients well with a hand mixer.

Cut the dates in small pieces and add them to the mix. Stir again.

Pour the mixture in a suitable small cake form (or a baking pan).

Stick the walnuts in the cake as well.

Finally, heat the oven at 180° C/ 356° F and bake the cake until fully cooked.

Wait for the dessert to cool off and spread some honey or maple syrup on top to add extra sweetness (if you desire).

Mini Cakes

Ingredients:

1/2 cup **Yogurt**
1/2 tsp. **Baking soda**
3 Tbsps. **Carob powder**
1 Tbsp. **Coconut butter** (soft)
1/2 cup **Rice flour**
1/2 cup **Millet flour**
A fistful of **Nuts of choice** (ground)
10 **Dates** (pitted)
1/2 cup **Maple syrup**

Instructions:

If the dates are too dry, soak them in some warm water for a couple of minutes and strain them.

Next, mix the yogurt with the baking soda and let it froth.

Consecutively, simply blend all ingredients until you reach a homogeneous mixture.

Start heating the oven to 180° C/ 356° F.

Finally, pour the batter in your favorite muffin (or mini pie) molds and bake the desserts until fully cooked.

You can place some baking paper inside the molds, if you wish to remove the cakes more easily after they cool down!

Mini Pies

Ingredients:

1 cup **Coconut flour**
1 cup **Gluten-free oat bran**
2 **Eggs**
1 cup **Butter** (melted)
1 tsp. **Baking soda**
Some **Coconut milk**
1/2 cup **Strawberries**
1-2 Tbsps. **Maple syrup**

Instructions:

First, place the strawberries in a metal pot, mash them with a fork, add the maple syrup, and heat them until they start to simmer and burble.

In the meantime, blend all the remaining ingredients in a kitchen robot.

Add as much coconut milk as to reach the consistency of thick pie dough.

Take small pie or muffin molds and place some of the mixture in.

Gently press to shape the crusts of the pies.

At this point, our strawberry jam should be ready.

Scoop some of it and fill the pies to the top.

Bake the desserts in a preheated oven (at 180° C/ 356° F) until they are fully cooked (the rims of the pie crusts must be nice and crunchy with a golden color).

Sponge Cake

Ingredients:

For the sponge cake:
4 **Eggs**
1/2 cup **Coconut sugar**
1/2 cup **Gluten-free flour mix**

For the cream:
1/2 cup **Coconut sugar**
3 Tbsps. **Corn starch** (non-GMO)
A pinch of **Salt**
1 tsp. **Vanilla extract**
1 1/2 cup **Milk**
1/2 cup **Cooking cream** (without sugar)
4 1/2 Tbsps. **Butter** (soft)
2-3 Tbsps. **Rum** (or some rum extract)
A few **Bananas** (optional)

Instructions:

Start by separating the egg yolks from the whites.

Beat the yolks, and mix them with the coconut sugar. When the sugar is fully melted, add the flour and blend again nicely.

In another container, whisk the egg whites until stiff.

Next, add them to the mixture and gently stir with a spatula or a spoon.

Heat the oven to 180° C/ 356° F and bake the cake until fully cooked (to a clean toothpick). You can use a baking tray covered with baking paper to easily remove the sponge afterwards.

Meanwhile, we can prepare the cream.

Place the milk and the cream in a metal pot and heat them on low temperature.

Next, mix the sugar with the corn starch, the salt, vanilla extract, some milk, and blend them well.

When the milk and cream mixture starts to simmer, slowly start pouring the sugary mass while stirring continuously.

Continue blending the ingredients for a minute or two, and take the pot off the heat.

Now we can add the butter, the rum, and we blend again thoroughly.

If the sponge cake is ready by now, take it out of the oven and leave it to cool down completely.

At this point, if you are using the bananas, you can cut them in slices.

Finally, we can start assembling the dessert.

Spread the cream all over the cake – cover as much space as possible – the top and the sides.

Decorate with the banana slices, if desired.

Feel free to sprinkle ground nuts or desiccated coconut, if you have any!

My notes:

Sponge Cake Roll with Yogurt Cream

Ingredients:

For the cake roll:
2 **Eggs**
1 cup **Yogurt**
A pinch of **Baking soda**
1/2 cup **Rice flour**
A pinch of **Salt**
1/4 tsp. **Vanilla powder**

For the cream:
1/2 cup **Buffalo yogurt**
1 **Banana**
1 tsp. **Lemon juice**
1/4 tsp. **Vanilla extract**

Instructions:

First, mix the yogurt and the baking soda in a bowl and stir.
Next, add the remaining ingredients for the roll and stir again. Remember to use a whisk, not a hand mixer, to blend the mixture.
Heat the oven at 180° C/ 356° F. Pour the batter in a flat baking pan covered with baking paper. Bake the dessert until fully cooked (use a toothpick to check if ready).
Next, take the sponge cake out of the oven and let it cool down nicely.
In the meantime, we can make the cream.

Peel the banana and cut it in medium chunks. Place it in a blender along with the remaining ingredients. Blend the mixture until fully homogenous.

Finally, spread the cream on top of the cake and roll it in to form a nice cake roll.

If you wish to make the cake creamier, make a bigger batch of the cream and cover the top of the dessert as well.

Gluten-free Cake with Apple and Walnuts

Ingredients:

3 **Eggs**
1 **Apple**
1/2 tsp. **Cinnamon**
1/2 tsp. **Macca powder**
1/2 tsp. **Baking powder**
1/2 cup **Ground walnuts** (or pecans)
1 tsp. **Goose fat**
Gluten-free flour mix of choice

Instructions:

First, remove the seeds from the apple and grate the fruit. You can use a kitchen chopper to make a puree more easily.

Next, beat the eggs in a large bowl.

Add the apple puree, the cinnamon, macca powder, baking powder, the ground nuts, and the fat.

Blend everything well until you have a nice homogeneous mass.

Start slowly adding some gluten-free flour until you reach a thick semi-liquid cake mixture. Remember to blend the batter well to remove any lumps.

If you like, you can decorate the cake with some apple slices, nuts, coconut shreds, or whatever you prefer.

Finally bake the dessert in a pre-heated oven (at 180° C/ 356° F) until fully cooked.

Summer Cake

Ingredients:

2 **Eggs**
1 **Banana**
3 Tbsps. **Coconut flour**
1 Tbsp. **Sesame tahini**
1 tsp. **Baking powder**
1 Tbsp. **Cocoa powder**
1 Tbsp. **Date molasses**
A fistful of **Ground nuts**
1 1/2 cup **High-fat yogurt**
Some **Fresh fruits and berries**

Instructions:

The preparation of this cake is extremely easy.

You can start by heating the oven to 200° C/ 392° F.

Next, beat the eggs in a large bowl.

Add all the remaining ingredients (except the yogurt and the berries) and blend them completely with a hand blender or a mixer.

Pour the batter in a flat baking pan and bake the dessert for about 15-20 minutes until fully cooked.

Leave the cake to cool down completely and cover it with the yogurt and decorate with the fruits on top.

Place the dessert in the fridge for a couple of hours for the cake to absorb the liquid from the yogurt and become softer and juicier!

Fruit Cake

Ingredients:

For the base:
4 Tbsps. **Ground hazelnuts**
6 Tbsps. **Rice flour**
1 1/2 Tbsp. **Cocoa powder**
3 1/2 Tbsps. **Coconut sugar**
3 Tbsps. **Rice bran oil**
1 **Egg**
Some **Water**

For the cream:
1/2 cup **Almond milk**
1/2 cup **Orange juice**
1 **Apple**
1 1/2 Tbsp. **Rice flour**
Some **Fruits of choice** – for decoration

Instructions:

Start heating the oven to 180° C/ 356° F.

Next, blend all ingredients for the base of the cake (except the water).

When the mixture is fully homogeneous, start adding the water in thin stream while stirring.

Add as much water as to reach nice and soft dough.

Next, take a baking tray and cover it with baking paper.

Roll the dough out evenly on the tray and bake the cake for about 10 minutes.

Meanwhile, we can prepare the cream.

Remove the seeds from the apple and grate the fruit. Alternatively, you can mince it in a kitchen chopper.

Next, place all ingredients for the cream in a metal pot and heat them on low temperature.

Keep stirring until the mixture starts to thicken.

Take it off the heat and leave it to cool down.

Finally, pour the cream on top of the cake and decorate with the desired fruits and berries.

Place the dessert in the fridge to stiffen a bit and maintain its form.

My notes:

GLUTEN-FREE SWEET BREADS, STRUDELS, AND TERRINES

Carrot Cheesecake

Ingredients:

For the base:
1 **Egg white**
1 **Carrot**
1 Tbsp. **Coconut flour**
1 **Date** (pitted)

For the cream:
3 1/2 Tbsps. **Cashew cheese**
1 **Egg**
1 tsp. **Vanilla extract**
1 Tbsp. **Maple syrup** (or a banana)
Some **Homemade sugar-free jam** (for topping)
Some **Coconut chips** (optional)

Instructions:

First, grate the carrot and blend it with the remaining ingredients for the base of the cheesecake in a kitchen chopper.

Next, heat the oven at 180° C/ 356° F, and bake the cake crust for 8-10 minutes until it hardens.

Now we can continue with the cream.

Simply blend all ingredients in a kitchen robot or a chopper until fully homogenous.

Next, cover the cake crust with the cream and bring it back in the oven for about 10 more minutes. The goal is for the cheesecake to start forming a gentle brown crust.

Finally, decorate with the homemade jam and sprinkle some coconut chips (if desired).

Store in the fridge to maintain its form.

If you are wondering how to make the sugar-free jam (or jelly), follow the next recipe. It is a wonderful preserve for the cold season!

Sugar-free Raspberry Winter Jam

Ingredients:

2 cups **Raspberries**
Some **Pure water**
1 1/2 Tbsp. **Gelatin**
Some **Maple syrup** – to taste (optional)
Glass jars with screw lids

Instructions:

Wash the raspberries and strain them from any excess liquid.

Place them in a metal pot along with some water. The liquid can be less or about half of the raspberries.

Heat the fruit mixture and stir well to blend it nicely.

When it starts to boil, take it off the heat to cool down a bit.

Now cover the gelatin with some water and wait for it to bulge up.

Next, heat it in a double boiler while stirring until it becomes transparent.

Consecutively, you can add the maple syrup to the raspberries, if you desire. If you skip the sweetener, the winter jam will become nicely sour. I personally like this taste, so I do not add any sweeteners at all.

Next, add the melted gelatin and stir well for a bit to blend all the ingredients.

While the mixture is still hot, pour it in the sterilized glass jars and tighten their lids.

Finally, turn the containers upside down to create vacuum.

When the jam is cooled down completely, flip the jars on their bottoms and place them in the fridge.

In several hours, the liquid will stiffen and gelatinize.

If you wish to liquefy it – simply warm it to room temperature.

Happy canning!

And here is the recipe for the vegan cheese you can prepare at home!

 *My notes:*

Vegan Cashew Cheese

Ingredients:

1 1/2 cup **Raw cashew**
1/2 **Lemon**
1/4 tsp. **Cheese starter** (or 1 capsule probiotic)
2 tsps. **Apple pectin**
Some **Himalayan salt** (to taste)
1/3 cup **Beer yeast flakes** (nutritional yeast)
Some **Coconut butter**

Instructions:

First, soak the cashew in some pure water for at least 4 hours, or leave it overnight.

When the nuts become nice and soft, strain them from the liquid and wash them thoroughly with clean water.

Next, transfer the cashew in a kitchen chopper or a robot; add the juice from the lemon, the apple pectin, beer flakes, salt, and the cheese starter. Blend everything well to form a homogenous mass.

Take a suitable container and oil it with the coconut butter – bottom and sides.

Place the cheese mixture inside and gently smoothen it with a kitchen knife.

Leave the vegan cheese in the fridge to harden a bit and it is ready for consumption.

At this point, it will be a bit soft and creamy. The more it rests and matures, the harder it will become.

Pear Strudel

Ingredients:

3 **Pears**
3 **Eggs**
A fistful of **Walnuts**
1/2 cup **Rice flour**
1/2 cup **Raisins**
1/2 cup **Yogurt**
1 tsp. **Baking soda**
2 Tbsps. **Flax seed flour**
1/3 cup **Coconut flour**
1/3 cup **Maple syrup** (stevia or agave)
1 tsp. **Vanilla extract**
1 tsp. **Cinnamon**

Instructions:

First, remove the seeds or stems from the pears. Dice the fruits in small cubes.

Next, mix the yogurt with the baking soda and stir.

While we wait for the yogurt mixture to start frothing, we can commence preparing the batter.

In a large bowl, beat the eggs, and mix them with the pears.

Next, add the yogurt and the remaining ingredients.

Stir well to blend everything well.

Start heating the oven at 180° C/ 356° F.

Take a flat baking tray and cover it with baking paper. Pour the strudel mixture in and bake for 30-40 minutes until fully cooked. You can check with a toothpick whether the cake is well baked.

Finally, wait for it to cool down completely and cut in the desired shapes.

Ice-cream Terrine

Ingredients:

1 1/2 cup **Dark chocolate** (preferably sugar-free)*
1/2 cup **Gluten-free cookies**
3-4 Tbsps. **Raisins**
1/2 cup **Rice flour**
1 cup **Milk**
2 **Eggs** (sanitized and from a trusted source)
1 tsp. **Baking soda**
3-4 Tbsps. **Cooking cream** (unsweetened)
2 Tbsps. **Coconut sugar** (or maple syrup)

Instructions:

Note: feel free to use any of the cookie recipes described below in this book – you will be sure they are 100% gluten-free and you will have full knowledge of all the other ingredients in them!

Let's begin!

First, make sure the eggs are at room temperature.

Place 1 cup of the chocolate and the milk in a double boiler to blend them completely.

Next, separate the egg yolks from the whites.

Beat the yolks and add them to the chocolate milk along with the coconut sugar and the cream.

Blend the ingredients well and take the mixture off the heat to cool down.

In the meantime, whisk the egg whites until stiff, chip the remaining chocolate in pieces, add them to the egg whites, and gently stir with a spoon or a spatula.

Next, take a suitable terrine mold and crush the cookies at its bottom to form the first layer of the dessert.

After that, pour the dairy mixture on the top of the biscuits and finally – the egg whites.

Place the ice-cream "cake" in the freezer for at least 20 minutes before consuming.

 *If you do not have sugar-free chocolate at your disposal, you can always make it on your own! You can find two of my favorite healthy chocolate recipes in my FREE ebook "12 Healthy Dessert Recipes"

My notes:

Chocolate Terrine

Ingredients:

1 cup **Dark chocolate** (preferably sugar-free)*
3/4 cup **Butter**
1/2 cup **Instant coffee** (or cocoa powder)
3/4 cup **Coconut sugar** (or maple syrup)
4 **Eggs**
2 fistfuls of **Fresh fruits of choice**

Instructions:

First, make sure the eggs are at room temperature.

Next, melt the chocolate along with the butter in a double boiler on low temperature.

When the brown mixture becomes completely homogeneous, add the coffee, the coconut sugar, and continue to blend the batter.

You can heat it to about 120° C/ 248° F. When the sugar is fully melted, take the mixture off the heat to cool down a bit.

In the meantime, start heating the oven to 180° C/ 356° F, and beat the eggs in a large bowl with a whisk.

Next, start slowly and gently adding the chocolate mixture to the eggs (in a thin stream) while continuously whisking and blending.

After that, place the fruits in the batter and stir with a spoon or a spatula. If they are too large, cut them in pieces beforehand.

Now take a terrine mold and cover it with baking paper. Pour the batter in and place the mold in a metal pan filled with water.

Bake the dessert in this double boiler for about 40 minutes.

Leave the terrine to cool down completely in the fridge overnight, and flip it upside down the next day!

 *If you do not have sugar-free chocolate at your disposal, you can always make it on your own! You can find two of my favorite healthy chocolate recipes in my FREE ebook "12 Healthy Dessert Recipes"

No Bake Chocolate Terrine with Plums

Ingredients:

2 **Eggs** (sanitized and from a trusted source)
3/4 cup **Dry plums** (not treated with sugar)
4 Tbsps. **Butter** (soft)
4 Tbsps. **Coconut sugar** (or maple syrup)
4 Tbsps. **Cognac** (or Amaretto, Nocino, etc.)
1/2 cup **Dark chocolate** (preferably sugar-free)*
1/2 cup **Cooking cream** (unsweetened)
1 Tbsp. **Cocoa powder**

Instructions:

Gently wash the plums and remove any pits, if any.

Mix them with the liquor and leave them to soak nicely until they soften (for about 3 hours). Alternatively, you can perform this step the night before.

Next, when the fruits are ready, cut them in medium pieces.

After that, melt the chocolate in a double boiler on low heat.

While you wait for the chocolate to cool down a bit, mix the butter with half of the sugar and the cocoa powder.

Next, separate the egg yolks from the whites.

Beat the yolks in a large cup and blend them with the remaining sugar.

After that, add the sweetened butter, the melted chocolate, and the plums.

In another container, beat the cream nicely with a whisk and add it to the batter.

Finally, take a terrine mold and place transparent kitchen foil inside.

Pour the batter in, cover it with more kitchen foil, and place the dessert in the freezer until it stiffens (about 3 hours).

When the terrine is ready, simply flip it upside down and enjoy!

 *If you do not have sugar-free chocolate at your disposal, you can always make it on your own! You can find two of my favorite healthy chocolate recipes in my FREE ebook "12 Healthy Dessert Recipes"

Sugar-free Sweet Easter Bread

Ingredients:

1 **Banana**
2 **Eggs**
3 Tbsps. **Yogurt**
1/2 tsp. **Baking soda**
1 Tbsp. **Liquid stevia***
1 Tbsp. **Coconut flour**
7 Tbsps. **Almond flour**
A fistful of **Raisins** (not treated with sugar)
Some **Cinnamon** (to taste)
1 tsp. **Carob powder**
1 tsp. **Vanilla extract**

Instructions:

First, mix the yogurt with the baking soda and leave it to froth for a bit.

In the meantime, separate the egg whites from the yolks.

Whisk the whites until stiff.

Next, mash the banana in a large bowl. Add the egg yolks, the yogurt, stevia extract, coconut flour, almond flour, the raisins, cinnamon, and the vanilla.

Blend the mixture thoroughly until it homogenizes.

Take another cup and place one tablespoon of the batter and the carob powder in it. Stir to blend them well.

Next, add the egg whites and gently homogenize the mixture with a spatula or a spoon.

At this point, you can start heating the oven at 180° C/ 356° F.

Take a bread mold and pour half of the mixture inside.

Next, gently add the carob mixture, and finally – pour the remaining of the batter.

Bake the Easter bread in the heated oven until fully cooked.

*The quantity of the stevia will depend on the type of product you use. Most extracts have a ratio to sugar as follows:

1 cup sugar = 1 tsp. liquid or powdered stevia

1 Tbsp. sugar = 1/4 tsp. powdered (6-9 drops liquid stevia)

1 tsp. sugar = a pinch of powdered (2-4 drops liquid stevia)

Keep in mind that there are other types of stevia extracts with different ratios, for example 1:1.

Eventually, experiment and see what quantities suit your taste best!

My notes:

Sweet Banana Bread (Cake)

Ingredients:

4 1/2 Tbsps. **Coconut butter** (melted)
1/2 cup **Maple syrup** (or agave, coconut sugar, stevia*, etc.)
2 **Eggs**
2 **Bananas**
4 Tbsps. **Milk**
1 Tbsp. **Baking soda**
1/2 tsp. **Cinnamon**
1/2 tsp. **Salt**
1 tsp. **Vanilla extract**
1 cup **Rice flour** (or gluten-free flour mix of choice)

Instructions:

First, beat the eggs in a large bowl and blend them with the maple syrup and the butter.

In another container, mash the bananas and transfer them to the main cake mixture.

Add the milk and stir again to homogenize the batter.

Next, add the baking soda, cinnamon, vanilla extract, the salt, and blend again.

Finally, slowly add the gluten-free flour as you continue to stir in order to reach a smooth homogenous consistency.

Heat the oven to 160° C - 170° C (320° F - 338° F) and bake the bread for about an hour until fully cooked.

*The quantity of the stevia will depend on the type of product you use. Most extracts have a ratio to sugar as follows:

1 cup sugar = 1 tsp. liquid or powdered stevia

1 Tbsp. sugar = 1/4 tsp. powdered (6-9 drops liquid stevia)

1 tsp. sugar = a pinch of powdered (2-4 drops liquid stevia)

Keep in mind that there are other types of stevia extracts with different ratios, for example 1:1.

Eventually, experiment and see what quantities suit your taste best!

Sweet Bread (Cake) with Pumpkin Cream

Ingredients:

For the cake:
2 **Eggs**
4 Tbsps. **Yogurt**
1 tsp. **Baking soda**
1 Tbsp. **Butter** (soft or melted)
1 Tbsp. **Carob powder**
7 **Dates** (pitted)
2 Tbsps. **Coconut flour**
1 tsp. **Rum extract** (adjust to taste)

For the cream:
1/2 cup **Cottage cheese** (or ricotta)
1 1/2 Tbsp. **Butter** (soft or melted)
1/2 cup **Sour cream**
1 cup **Pumpkin** (boiled, steamed, or roasted)
1 Tbsp. **Honey** (or maple syrup, coconut sugar, etc.)
1 tsp. **Gelatin**
Some **Cold water** (to cover the gelatin)
Some **Ground raw nuts** (hazelnuts, almonds, walnuts, etc.)
1 tsp. **Carob powder**

Instructions:

First, we will prepare the base for our cake.

Mix the yogurt with the baking soda and leave it to froth for a bit.

Next, place the eggs, the butter, the bubbly yogurt, and the dates in a blender (or a kitchen robot) and mince them well.

Consecutively, add the carob powder, the coconut flour, and the rum extract and blend the mixture once again.

Start heating the oven to 180° C/ 356° F.

Transfer the batter in a bread baking pan (about 7"x3") and bake in the pre-heated furnace for about 20 minutes (or until fully cooked).

Meanwhile, we can start making the cream.

First, place the gelatin in a small cup and cover it with cold water.

While you wait for the gelatin to bulge up, mix the cottage cheese with the butter and blend them well with a hand mixer (or a blender).

Place the gelatin in a double boiler and warm it until it becomes transparent.

Next, leave it aside to cool down a bit.

In the meantime, add the sour cream, the pumpkin, honey, and the nuts to the cottage cheese, and homogenize the mixture once again.

After that, add the gelatin and stir again nicely.

Divide the cream into two equal parts, and mix one half with the carob powder (1 tsp.).

Finally, when the cake is cooked and cooled down completely, cover it with both creams and store it in the fridge for a couple of hours to maintain its shape.

My notes:

GLUTEN-FREE MUFFINS
AND BROWNIES

Muffins with Plums

Ingredients:

3 **Eggs**
3-4 Tbsps. **Sugar beet syrup**
2 Tbsps. **Sesame tahini**
1/2 cup **Sour cream**
1/2 tsp. **Baking soda**
2 Tbsps. **Butter** (melted)
1/2 cup **Gluten-free flour mix**
1/2 cup **Ground walnuts**
Some **Plums** – to taste

Instructions:

Take as many plums as you like, depending on how many chunks of fruit you like to have in the muffins.

Pit the fruits and cut them in small pieces.

Next, mix the sour cream with the baking soda and stir well.

In another bowl, whisk the eggs, and add the beet syrup, the tahini, butter, walnuts, and the sour cream.

Stir everything well to form a homogenous mixture. Add most of the cut plums and leave some of them for decoration. Stir the batter again.

Now it is time to heat the oven at 180° C/ 356° F.

Next, pour the muffin mixture in the molds and cover with the remaining plums.

Bake the desserts until fully cooked – about 25 minutes.

Blueberry Muffins

Ingredients:

3 **Eggs**
1 **Banana** (fully ripe)
1/2 cup **Dates** (pitted)
1 Tbsp. **Sesame tahini**
2 Tbsps. **Butter** (melted)
1/2 cup **Yogurt**
1/2 tsp. **Baking soda**
1/2 cup **Gluten-free flour mix of choice**
2 Tbsps. **Coconut flour**
2 fistfuls of **Blueberries**

Instructions:

Place the eggs along with the remaining ingredients (except the blueberries) in a kitchen robot or a blender.

Blend the mixture well until it is fully homogenous.

Next, pour the batter in a large bowl and add the blueberries. Gently stir with a spatula to distribute the fruits evenly.

Oil the muffin molds and fill them with the mixture.

Bake the desserts in a preheated oven at 180° C/ 356° F for about 25 minutes.

Blueberry Fiber Muffins

Ingredients:

6 **Eggs**
1/2 cup **Dates** (pitted)
2 tsps. **Psyllium husk**
2 tsps. **Ground flax seeds**
3 1/2 Tbsps. **Water**
3 1/2 Tbsps. **Coconut flour**
1/2 tsp. **Baking powder**
1/2 cup **Blueberries**

Instructions:

First, mix the ground flax seeds with the water and wait for them to form their jelly.

Next, add the husk and stir again.

Place the eggs and the dates in a kitchen chopper and blend them completely.

Now add the fiber mixture to the eggs and dates and stir again.

Next, add the flour and the baking powder and blend the mixture until it becomes fully homogenous. If it seems too dry and difficult to stir, add more water or any milk of choice.

Finally, add the blueberries and stir with a spoon or a spatula.

Start heating the oven to 170° C/338° F.

Pour the batter in the muffin molds and bake for about 20 minutes!

That's it!

Coconut Muffins I

Ingredients:

3 **Eggs**
5-6 Tbsps. **Coconut sugar**
1 cup **Desiccated coconut**
1 cup **Coconut milk**

Instructions:

Mix the eggs with the sugar and blend well with a hand mixer.

Next, add the coconut shreds, the milk, and blend again.

Leave the mixture to rest for about 15 minutes for the desiccated coconut to absorb some of the liquid.

Pour the batter in muffin molds and bake in a preheated oven at 170° C/338° F for 15 minutes (or until ready).

My notes:

Coconut Muffins II

Ingredients:

4 **Eggs**
5 Tbsps. **Coconut flour**
2 cups **Milk**
2 Tbsps. **Maple syrup**
2 Tbsps. **Desiccated coconut**
Some **Raspberries and Blueberries** (for decorating)

Instructions:

Combine all the ingredients well to form a homogenous mixture.

Use a hand mixer to simplify the process.

If needed, adjust the consistency of the batter by adding more coconut flour or milk.

Pour the mixture in muffin molds, decorate with the fruits, and bake at 200° C/ 392° F until fully cooked.

My notes:

Pumpkin Muffins

Ingredients:

2 **Eggs**
2 1/2 Tbsps. **Desiccated coconut**
1 cup **Boiled** (steamed or roasted) **pumpkin**
3 Tbsps. **Butter**
4 Tbsps. **Pumpkin seed tahini**
1/2 cup **Buffalo yogurt** (or cottage cheese)
1 tsp. **Baking powder**
Some **Mashed white cheese** (optional)

Instructions:

Simply blend all ingredients well in a blender or a kitchen robot.

If you wish to make the desserts a bit salty, add some white cheese.

Pour the mixture in the muffin molds and heat the oven at 180° C/ 356° F.

Bake the desserts for about 30 minutes, or until fully cooked.

My notes:

Chocolate Muffins with Sweet Potato

Ingredients:

1 **Sweet potato** (large)
1/2 cup **Maple syrup**
5 Tbsps. **Coconut butter** (melted)
1 1/2 tsp. **Vanilla extract**
1/2 cup **Rice milk**
1 cup **Chickpea flour**
1 cup **Coconut flour**
1/4 tsp. **Salt**
4 tsps. **Baking powder** (gluten-free)
3-4 Tbsps. **Cocoa powder**
1/2 cup **Dark chocolate** (sugar-free)*

Instructions:

First, peel the sweet potato, cut it in small pieces and boil it until it softens.

Next, strain it and mash it nicely with a fork.

Add the maple syrup, the coconut butter, vanilla extract, and the rice milk. Blend everything well.

In another container, mix the dry ingredients – chickpea flour, coconut flour, salt, baking powder, and the cocoa powder. Stir well to blend them as well.

Next, combine both mixtures and use a hand mixer to homogenize the batter completely until it forms thick dough.

Melt the chocolate in a double boiler and prepare the muffin molds (about 12 pieces).

Place a paper cupcake cup in each muffin mold and one tablespoon of the dough.

Next, pour one tablespoon of the melted chocolate in each cup, and divide the remaining dough in each muffin cup.

Now it is time to heat the oven at 200° C/ 392° F and bake the desserts for 8 minutes. Finally, lower the temperature to 180° C/ 356° F and continue cooking the muffins for 10-15 more minutes.

*If you do not have sugar-free chocolate at your disposal, you can always make it on your own! You can find two of my favorite healthy chocolate recipes in my FREE ebook "12 Healthy Dessert Recipes"

Flour-less Muffins

Ingredients:

3 **Bananas** (fully ripe)
4 Tbsps. **Maple syrup**
1 Tbsp. **Cocoa powder**
1 tsp. **Vanilla extract**
3 **Eggs**
1/2 tsp. **Baking powder**
4 1/2 Tbsps. **Ground walnuts**
Some **Olive oil**

Instructions:

Mash the bananas and beat the eggs.

Next, simply combine the banana puree with the maple syrup, the eggs, cocoa powder, vanilla extract, and the baking powder.

Blend everything well with a hand mixer to homogenize the batter.

Next, add the ground walnuts and stir again with a spoon or a spatula.

Oil the muffin molds with some olive oil and pour the mixture in.

Heat the oven at 180° C/ 356° F and bake the desserts for about 20-25 minutes. The time will depend on your oven and whether you use the fan-assist function or not.

Pulp Muffins

Ingredients:

1 cup **Carrot pulp**
1/2 cup **Apple pulp**
1/2 cup **Butter** (soft)
1 cup **Dates** (pitted)
4 **Eggs**
5 Tbsps. **Buffalo yogurt**
2 tsps. **Baking soda**
2 Tbsps. **Coconut flour**
1 Tbsp. **Rice flour**
1/2 cup **Ground walnuts**
Some **Water**

Instructions:

First, mix the baking soda with the yogurt, stir and let the mixture froth for a bit.

Next, place all ingredients (except the walnuts) in a kitchen robot (or a blender) and mince them well. Add as much water as to reach a thick cake mixture consistency.

After that, add the walnuts and stir with a spoon.

Heat the oven at the usual 180° C/ 356° F and bake the muffins for about 40 minutes.

Wait for the desserts to cool off completely and remove them from the molds.

No-bake Cocoa Oatmeal Muffins

Ingredients:

1 cup **Gluten-free oatmeal**
2 Tbsps. **Cocoa powder**
1 cup **Butter**
1 cup **Ground walnuts**
1/2 cup **Molasses**
1 tsp. **Vanilla extract**

Instructions:

First, melt the butter and mix it with the molasses. Blend them well.

Next, in another bowl, mix the oatmeal with the cocoa powder.

Transfer the oatmeal mixture to the butter and molasses, and blend them well.

Finally, add the walnuts and the vanilla extract, and stir one more time.

Place some of the mixture in muffin molds and put them in the fridge. The butter will stiffen and keep the form of the muffins.

Note: if you wish to improve the taste of the oatmeal and the walnuts, you can roast them in a non-stick pan for several minutes before preparing the desserts.

Raspberry Cupcakes

Ingredients:

For the cupcakes:
3 **Eggs**
4 Tbsps. **Sesame flour**
4 Tbsps. **Coconut flour**
15 **Dates** (pitted)
1 **Banana**
1 Tbsp. **Hazelnut tahini**
1 cup **Yogurt**
A pinch of **Baking soda**

For the filling:
1 cup **Cottage cheese** (or ricotta cheese)
3 Tbsps. **Butter** (soft)
4-5 Tbsps. **Maple syrup**
2 Tbsps. **Coconut milk**
Some **Desiccated coconut**
1 cup **Raspberries**

Instructions:

First, we are going to prepare the cupcakes.

Start by separating the egg whites from the yolks.

Next, whisk the egg whites until stiff.

Place the yolks in a blender along with the dates, and blend them well.

Add the banana, the hazelnut tahini, and blend again.

Next, mix the yogurt with the baking soda and leave it to froth for a bit.

Add the yogurt mixture in the blender and continue to homogenize the batter.

After that, you can transfer the mixture in a large cup, and add the flours – sesame and coconut.

Stir again with a hand mixer.

Consecutively, add the egg whites, and very gently blend the batter with a spatula or a spoon. Leave the mixture to rest for about 20 minutes.

Meanwhile we can start making the raspberry filling.

Blend the cottage cheese with the butter, maple syrup, and the coconut milk.

Add the raspberries and stir again to homogenize the mixture.

Finally, add the desiccated coconut to thicken the cream – add as much as you like until you reach the desired consistency.

At this point, you can start heating the oven to 180° C/ 356° F.

Now take your muffin molds and place a cupcake paper in each one of them. Grease them with some butter in order to be easier to remove the paper later on.

Start filling the cupcakes by pouring 1 tablespoon of the batter.

Next, put 1 tablespoon of the raspberry cream on top, and finally – cover with some more of the cupcake mixture.

Place the desserts in the baking tray and bake until fully cooked.

Chocolate Brownies

Ingredients:

1 cup **Dark chocolate** (sugar-free)*
1 cup **Butter**
1 cup **Dates** (pitted)
4 **Eggs**
2 tsps. **Vanilla extract**
1/2 cup **Sweet chestnut flour**
A pinch of **Himalayan salt**
Some **Sugar-free chocolate chips** (optional)

Instructions:

Start by melting the chocolate and the butter in a double boiler.

In the meantime, you can grind the dates in a kitchen chopper until you reach a homogenous puree.

Next, when the chocolate and the butter are fully melted and blended, take them off the heat.

Combine the dark chocolate mousse with the dates and stir well.

In another container, beat the eggs, and transfer them to the mixture.

Add the vanilla extract and start blending the ingredients gently with a spoon or a spatula.

Next, add the chestnut flour and the salt, and continue to stir.

Now we can start heating the oven at 180° C/ 356° F. If you are using the fan-assist function, set the temperature at 160° C/ 320° F.

Consecutively, take a flat baking tray (preferably 13" x 9"), grease it with some butter, and cover it with baking paper.

Pour the batter in and bake the cake for about 30 minutes.

If you are using the chocolate chips, take the tray out of the oven at the 15th minute and shove them gently inside the dessert.

Finally, bring the cake back, and wait for it to bake completely. Take it out, leave it to cool down, and cut in the desired forms.

*If you do not have sugar-free chocolate at your disposal, you can always make it on your own! You can find two of my favorite healthy chocolate recipes in my FREE ebook "12 Healthy Dessert Recipes"

My notes:

Flour-less Brownie

Ingredients:

For the base:
1/2 cup **Ground almonds** (raw)
1/2 cup **Ground hazelnuts** (raw)
1/2 cup **Coconut flour**
1/2 cup **Yam flour**
1 cup **Coconut sugar**
2 **Eggs**
1-2 Tbsps. **Cocoa powder**

For the icing:
1 Tbsp. **Ground hazelnuts** (raw)
1 Tbsp. **Cocoa powder**
1 Tbsp. **Coconut butter**
1 Tbsp. **Coconut sugar**
Some **Water**

Instructions:

Mix the dry ingredients for the base of the brownie in a large cup – the ground almonds, hazelnuts, coconut flour, yam flour, cocoa powder, and the coconut sugar.

Stir well to blend them.

Next, separate the egg yolks from the whites. Whisk the egg yolks, and beat the egg whites until stiff in another cup.

Combine the dry ingredients with the egg yolks and the egg whites and gently stir with a spatula or a spoon.

Pour the mixture in a baking tray covered with baking paper.

Heat the oven at 180° C/ 356° F and bake the brownie for about 25 minutes.

In the meantime, we can prepare the topping.

Melt the butter, if not already.

Mix it with the cocoa powder, the ground hazelnuts, and the coconut sugar.

Blend the ingredients well, and add some water until you reach the desired creamy consistency.

Continue to stir until the sugar melts completely.

When the brownie is fully cooked, wait for it to cool down completely, and cover it with the icing.

Bon Appetite!

Apple Brownie

Ingredients:

For the base:
2/3 cup **Buckwheat flakes**
1 cup **Ground almonds** (raw or blanched)
4 Tbsps. **Apple flour**
2 **Large apples**
2 Tbsps. **Butter** (soft)
1 tsp. **Almond extract**
Some **Date molasses** – to taste
Some **Water** (for the apples)

For the icing:

2 Tbsps. **Hazelnut tahini**

2 Tbsps. **Sesame tahini**

2 Tbsps. **Honey** (or adjust to taste)

1 Tbsp. **Cocoa powder** (or carob powder)

3 1/2 – 4 Tbsps. **Coconut butter**

1/2 cup **Coconut cream**

Instructions:

First, cut the apples in quarters and boil them in some water until they soften.

Next, when the fruits cool down, remove the seeds and cut them in small pieces.

Important: do not throw away the apple broth – we will need it later in the recipe!

Consecutively, mix all ingredients for the base of the brownie in a kitchen robot, a chopper or a blender.

Blend them well and add some of the apple water to reach the desired consistency – a thick mass.

Start heating the oven to the usual 180° C/ 356° F.

Next, pour the cake batter in a baking pan (approx. 11" x 7") covered with baking paper.

Cook for about 40-45 minutes until fully baked.

In the meantime, we can make the topping.

Place all the components for the cream in a double boiler and blend them on low heat.

Remember to keep the temperature below 98.6°F (37°C) to preserve the beneficial nutrients in the honey.

Otherwise, you can use maple syrup, or wait for the cream to cool down a bit before adding the bee product!

When the brownie is ready and nicely chilled, remove it from the baking pan and cover with the tahini topping!

Pulp Brownie

Ingredients:

1 cup **Pulp of choice** (carrot, apple, etc.)
2 **Eggs**
3 Tbsps. **Coconut butter**
3 Tbsps. **Coconut flour**
1 Tbsp. **Date molasses**
1 Tbsp. **Cocoa powder**
1 tsp. **Baking powder**
Chocolate chips – for decoration (optional)

Instructions:

Start heating the oven to 200° C/ 392° F.

Next, simply combine all ingredients in a kitchen chopper or a robot.

Blend them completely until you reach a homogenous mass.

Pour the mixture in a suitable rectangular baking mold and cook the dessert for about 20-30 minutes.

Take the brownie out of the oven and cover it with the chocolate chips until it's still hot.

Pumpkin Brownie

Ingredients:

1 cup **Pumpkin**
3 1/2 Tbsps. **Flax seed flour**
5-6 **Dates** (pitted) – adjust to taste
4 **Eggs**
10 **Cocoa beans**
1 tsp. **Cinnamon**

Instructions:

This is a very simple recipe, so you can start heating the oven (180° C/ 356° F) right away!

Next, cut the pumpkin in medium pieces and place it in a kitchen chopper (or a robot).

Add the remaining ingredients and blend them well.

Take a flat (rectangular) baking pan and cover it with baking paper.

Pour the brownie mixture in and bake for about 30-35 minutes (until fully cooked).

When the dessert is ready, leave it in the pan to cool down completely, and then you can remove it and slice it in pieces.

My notes:

Coconut Brownie with Chocolate Topping

Ingredients:

For the brownie:
2 **Eggs**
5 Tbsps. **Cocoa powder**
5 1/2 Tbsps. **Butter**
1/2 cup **Coconut sugar**
A pinch of **Salt**
1/2 cup **Almond flour**

For the cream:
1 cup **Cottage cheese**
1/2 cup **Unsweetened condensed milk**
1 cup **Cooking cream** (unsweetened)
2 Tbsps. **Butter**
1 tsp. **Vanilla extract**
1/2 cup **Desiccated coconut**
Some **Honey** (or maple syrup) – to taste
2 sheets **Gelatin** (or 1 tsp. powdered gelatin)

For the chocolate topping:
4 Tbsps. **Coconut butter**
5 Tbsps. **Cocoa powder**
5 Tbsps. **Honey**
1 tsp. **Vanilla extract**
Some **Cooking cream** (unsweetened)

Instructions:

First, we start with the base for the brownie.

Beat the eggs in a suitable cup or a bowl.

Next, place the butter, the cocoa powder, and the coconut sugar in a metal pot and heat them on low temperature.

When the butter melts completely and the mixture becomes fully homogeneous, take the pot off the heat and let it cool down a bit.

In the meantime, start heating the oven to 180° C/ 356° F.

Consecutively, slowly and gently add the eggs, the salt, and the almond flour. Remember that the temperature of the mixture needs to be close to the eggs', so that they won't coagulate!

Stir well to blend the ingredients, pour the batter in a flat baking pan, and bake in the pre-heated oven until fully cooked. Check with a toothpick whether the cake is ready. It may take about 15-20 minutes.

Meanwhile, we can make the cream.

Place the milk, the butter, and the cream in a metal pot and heat them on low temperature.

When everything is fully melted and homogenized, add the desiccated coconut as well.

Stir well and take the pot off the heat.

Add your sweetener of choice, but remember that if you are using honey, you need to wait for the mixture to cool down below body temperature first!

Next, add the cottage cheese and the vanilla extract, and blend the cream completely (use a hand blender or a mixer).

Add the gelatin sheets, stir again, and place the cream in the fridge to stiffen.

The preparation of the chocolate topping is very easy – simply blend all ingredients and add as much cooking cream as to form the desired creamy consistency. And that's it!

Now we can assemble the dessert!

When the brownie has cooled down completely, cover it with the coconut cream.

Put it in the fridge for an hour to settle and maintain its shape.

Finally, cover with the chocolate and place the brownie back in the refrigerator until serving!

Cocoa Mini Cakes

Ingredients:

1 **Banana**
3 **Eggs**
3 Tbsps. **High-fat yogurt** (like buffalo)
2 Tbsps. **Coconut flour**
4-5 Tbsps. **Cocoa powder**
1 tsp. **Baking powder**
10 **Dates** (pitted)
1 tsp. **Vanilla extract**
1/2 tsp. **Nutmeg**
Some **Cocoa butter** (melted)
Some **Ground walnuts** (for decoration)

Instructions:

First, mash the banana with a fork.

Next, beat the eggs in another cup, and add them to the fruit puree.

Place the yogurt in a kitchen chopper (or a robot), add the dates, and blend them well to form a homogenous mass. Transfer the mixture to the eggs and the banana.

In another bowl, mix the dry ingredients – the coconut flour, cocoa powder, baking powder, nutmeg, and stir well.

Combine the flours with the main mixture, add the vanilla extract, and blend completely.

Take out some muffin molds (about 6) and oil them with the cocoa butter.

Divide the cake mixture into the cups and sprinkle some ground walnuts on top.

Bake the desserts at 180° C/ 356° F until fully cooked. You can check with a toothpick to see if the desserts are ready.

Mini Carob Cakes

Ingredients:

3 **Eggs**
1 cup **Coconut sugar** (maple syrup, pitted dates, etc.)
1/2 cup **Olive oil**
1/2 cup **Yogurt**
2 tsps. **Baking powder**
1 tsp. **Vanilla extract**
1 1/2 cup **Carob powder**

Instructions:

The preparation of these delicious mini cakes is very easy!

First, switch on the oven at 180° C/ 356° F while we prepare the desserts.

Start by beating the eggs in a large bowl.

Add the coconut sugar and continue to stir with a hand mixer or a blender.

Gently add the olive oil, the yogurt, baking powder, vanilla extract while still blending the batter.

Finally, add the carob powder and stir the mixture nicely once again.

Pour the batter in small muffin molds and bake them until fully cooked.

Remember to check with a toothpick if the desserts are ready!

My notes:

Mini Pies with Plum Jam

Ingredients:

For the pies:
2 **Eggs**
1/2 cup **Sesame flour**
3 1/2 Tbsps. **Coconut flour**
2 Tbsps. **Apple flour**
20 **Dates** (pitted)
1 **Large apple**
1 cup **Yogurt**
1 tsp. **Baking soda**
1/2 tsp. **Cinnamon**
1/2 tsp. **Cloves** (ground)
1/2 tsp. **Ginger powder**
3-4 Tbsps. **Butter**

For the jam:
10 **Plums**
3 Tbsps. **Maple syrup** (or coconut sugar to taste)
Some **Water**
Some **Ghee** – optional
Some **Desiccated coconut** - optional

Instructions:

First, we will start with the jam since it needs a bit more time.

Pit the plums and grind them in a chopper.

Next, transfer them to a metal pot, and cover them with some water.

Heat the fruits on low temperature and stir sporadically.

While we wait for some of the water to evaporate, we can continue with the pies.

Peel the apple, remove its seeds, dice it in small cubes, and boil it.

When it becomes nice and soft, simply puree it with a masher or a hand blender.

If the plum jam is starting to thicken, add the maple syrup, and stir well until it dissolves completely. At this point, you can add some ghee butter to make the jelly smoother, if you wish.

Next, take the sweetness off the heat and leave it aside.

Now we can continue with the pies.

Take a large bowl and place the flours in it – sesame flour, coconut flour, and the apple flour. Add the spices (cinnamon, ginger, cloves) and stir well to blend.

Next, mix the yogurt with the baking soda, stir, and wait for a bit until it starts to froth.

Place the eggs, the bubbly yogurt, and the apple puree in a blender, and mince them well.

Now transfer the liquid mixture to the flour mix and gently blend with a hand blender or a mixer.

Add the ghee and continue to homogenize the batter. If the butter is too hard, heat it a bit for it to soften.

Consecutively, we can start assembling the pies.

Take your favorite muffin or cupcake molds, grease them with some butter, and place some of the batter inside.

Make medium sized holes in the center of each cup and fill it with the plum jam.

If you wish, you can garnish the desserts with some desiccated coconut.

Heat the oven at 180° C/ 356° F and bake the pies until they are fully cooked.

Leave them to cool down completely and remove from the molds!

My notes:

GLUTEN-FREE COOKIES AND BISCUITS

Simple Biscuits

Ingredients:

2 cups **Fine gluten-free oatmeal**
1 tsp. **Cinnamon**
1/4 tsp. **Vanilla powder**
1 **Apple**
A fistful of **Raisins**

Instructions:

Peel the apple, remove its seeds and grind it in a kitchen chopper.

Next, simply combine all ingredients and blend them with a spoon.

Leave the mixture to rest for about 30 minutes.

Next, take a baking tray and cover it with baking paper.

Form the biscuits with the spoon and bake at 180° C/ 356° F for about 20 minutes.

Voila!

My notes:

Golden Rice Biscuits

Ingredients:

2 **Egg yolks**
2 Tbsps. **Coconut butter** (melted)
4 Tbsps. **Date molasses**
1 tsp. **Baking powder**
1 tsp. **Vanilla extract**
1/2 cup **Rice flour**

Instructions:

First, beat the egg yolks and mix them with the coconut butter. Stir well to blend the ingredients and get a nice homogenous fluffy mixture.

Next, add the date syrup, the vanilla extract, and blend again.

In another container, mix the rice flour and the baking powder, and stir well to homogenize them completely.

Now you can transfer the flour to the sweet mixture, and stir again with a fork (or a whisk).

Next, start heating the oven at 170° C/338° F.

In the meantime, take a baking tray and cover it with baking paper.

Start forming small balls from the soft cookie dough and placing them in the tray. Now press gently with the fork to flatten the biscuits.

Finally, bake for 12-15 minutes.

Ginger Cookies

Ingredients:

For the dough:
3 1/2 cups **Gluten-free flour mix**
1/2 tsp. **Baking soda**
1 tsp. **Cinnamon**
1/2 tsp. **Nutmeg**
1/2 cup **Butter** (soft)
2 1/2 tsps. **Fresh ginger**
1/2 cup **Maple syrup** (or agave)
15 **Dates** (pitted)
1 **Egg**
3 Tbsps. **Almond tahini**

For the icing:
1 **Egg white**
A pinch of **Baking powder**
Some **Xylitol** (to taste)

Instructions:

In a bowl, mix the flour, baking soda, the cinnamon, and the nutmeg. Stir well to blend them.

Next, cut the butter in cubes and add it to the dry ingredients.

Peel and grate the ginger, and add it to the mixture.

Take a kitchen chopper and puree the dates along with the egg, the almond tahini, and the maple syrup.

Next, transfer the sweet mixture to the flour and butter.

Start blending and kneading the dough. If you have a kitchen robot, you can use it to simplify this task and save you some time.

Consecutively, place the dough between two baking paper sheets and roll it out until you reach a thickness of about 0.2" (5 mm). Cut out the cookies with the desired shapes and they are ready for baking.

Heat the oven at about 150°-160° C/ 302°-320° F and bake the cookies for 14-15 minutes (you can use the fan-assist option, if you have one).

Let the desserts cool down on a grid.

In the meantime, we can prepare the icing.

Whisk the egg white until stiff and mix with the baking soda and the xylitol.

Finally, garnish the cookies with the cream. You can use a cream syringe, if you have one.

Bon Appetite!

Almond Cookies

Ingredients:

1 cup **Almond flour**
1 Tbsp. **Coconut butter** (melted)
1 **Egg**
2 Tbsps. **Liquid stevia***
1 1/2 tsp. **Vanilla extract**
1 tsp. **Cinnamon**
Some **Flaked almonds** (for decoration)

Instructions:

Simply mix all the ingredients (except the flaked almonds) in a large bowl and blend them well.

Take a baking tray and cover it with baking paper.

Scoop some of the cookie dough to form small balls with your hands.

Next, place them on the tray and gently press them to make them flatter. Cover the desserts with the shredded almonds.

Finally, heat the oven at 180° C/ 356° F and bake for about 15-20 minutes. You can use the fan-assist option of your oven, if you have one.

*The quantity of the stevia will depend on the type of product you use. Most extracts have a ratio to sugar as follows:

1 cup sugar = 1 tsp. liquid or powdered stevia

1 Tbsp. sugar = 1/4 tsp. powdered (6-9 drops liquid stevia)

1 tsp. sugar = a pinch of powdered (2-4 drops liquid stevia)

Keep in mind that there are other types of stevia extracts with different ratios, for example 1:1.

Eventually, experiment and see what quantities suit your taste best!

Walnut Cookies I

Ingredients:

1 cup **Walnuts**
3 **Eggs**
1/2 cup **Dates** (pitted)

Instructions:

This recipe is very easy and quick, so you can start heating the oven at 200° C/ 392° F.

Next, place the walnuts in a kitchen chopper and grind them.

Add the eggs and the dates and continue to blend the mixture until it becomes fully homogenous.

Take a baking tray and cover it baking paper.

Scoop some of the cookie dough and form small spheres.

Place them in the tray and gently press to flatten the biscuits.

Place the cookies in the oven and immediately lower the temperature to 160° C/ 320° F.

Bake until the delicious desserts are fully cooked and nicely crunchy.

Walnut Cookies II

Ingredients:

1/2 cup **Walnuts**
2 Tbsps. **Sunflower tahini**
1 Tbsp. **Date molasses** (syrup)
1 **Egg**

Instructions:

The preparation of this recipe is almost identical with the previous one!

Start heating the oven – this time to 180° C/ 356° F.

Grind the walnuts in a kitchen chopper, and add the remaining ingredients.

Blend the mixture and form the cookies as usual.

Arrange them in a baking tray covered with baking paper and bake for about 15-18 minutes until fully cooked.

When the cookies are ready, take them out, leave them to cool down completely, and store them in a tightly sealed jar.

My notes:

Chocolate Mint Cookies

Ingredients:

1/2 cup **Wholegrain rice flour**
2 **Eggs**
3 1/2 Tbsps. **Dark chocolate** (sugar-free)*
1 tsp. **Baking powder**
1/4 tsp. **Vanilla extract**
3 sprigs **Mint**
1 tsp. **Ghee** (or coconut butter)
1-2 Tbsps. **Date molasses**

Instructions:

Simply mix all ingredients well and blend them completely.

Form small biscuits on a baking tray covered with baking paper.

Heat the oven at 200° C/ 392° F and bake the cookies for 10 minutes.

Easy peasy!

*If you do not have sugar-free chocolate at your disposal, you can always make it on your own! You can find two of my favorite healthy chocolate recipes in my FREE ebook "12 Healthy Dessert Recipes"

Coconut Cookies

Ingredients:

1 cup **Coconut flour**

1 1/2 Tbsp. **Corn flour** (non-GMO)

2 Tbsps. **Coconut butter**

2 **Bananas**

2 **Eggs**

Instructions:

Beat the eggs in a large bowl, and mix them with the bananas and the coconut butter.

If the butter is too hard, heat it for a bit to become soft and pliable.

Blend the mixture well, and add the remaining ingredients.

Stir again to homogenize the mixture.

Leave the dough to rest for about 10 minutes.

In the meantime, heat the oven at 200° C/ 392° F.

Next, take a baking tray and cover it with baking paper.

Take a spoon and scoop from the cookie dough to form small balls.

Place the desserts in the tray and gently press in order for them to become flatter.

Bake for 15 minutes and voila!

Blueberry Cookies

Ingredients:

2 **Bananas**
10 **Dates** (pitted)
2-3 Tbsps. **Blueberry jam** (preferably homemade and sugar-free)
1 cup **Coconut milk**
1 cup **Apple flour**
1/2 cup **Rice flour**
1/2 tsp. **Baking powder**
1 Tbsp. **Chia**
2-3 Tbsps. **Coconut butter** (melted)
4 1/2 Tbsps. **Ground hazelnuts**
1-2 tsps. **Vanilla extract**
2-3 fistfuls of **Fresh Blueberries**

Instructions:

Start heating the oven to 180° C/ 356° F.

In the meantime, we will prepare the cookie dough since the procedure is very easy and quick.

Cut the bananas in medium pieces and place them in a kitchen robot or a blender.

Add the remaining ingredients (except the whole blueberries) and blend them well until they fully homogenize.

Add the fresh berries and gently stir with a spoon or a spatula to distribute them evenly.

Take a baking tray and cover it baking paper.

Form the cookies as usual – shape them as small spheres and press gently to flatten the biscuits.

Bake for about 20-30 minutes until they are fully cooked and ready!

Enjoy!

Avocado Cookies

Ingredients:

1/2 cup **Avocado** (ripe)

1/2 cup **Coconut sugar**

1/2 tsp. **Vanilla extract**

1 tsp. **Apple cider vinegar**

1/2 tsp. **Baking powder**

2 Tbsps. **Cocoa powder**

1 tsp. **Cinnamon**

3/4 cup **Gluten-free flour mix of choice**

1/2 cup **Dark chocolate chips** (preferably sugar-free)

Instructions:

Begin by heating the oven to 180° C/ 356° F.

Next, mash the avocado and blend it with the sugar.

Consecutively, add the vanilla extract, cinnamon, the apple cider vinegar, cocoa powder, the baking powder, and stir again nicely.

Finally, add the flour and blend completely until the mixture becomes fully homogenous.

Add the chocolate chips and stir again with a spoon.

Shape the cookies as usual – scoop some of the dough, place the balls on the baking tray (covered with baking paper), and press them.

154 · Milica Vladova

Bake the desserts for 15-20 minutes until they are well cooked.

Leave them to cool down completely before sealing them in your favorite cookie jar!

Cinnamon Cookies with Cottage Cheese

Ingredients:

1/2 cup **Cottage cheese** (curd)
1/2 cup **Gluten-free oatmeal**
1/2 cup **Apples** (or 2 small ones)
3 1/2 Tbsps. **Olive oil**
1 Tbsp. **Maple syrup**
3 tsps. **Cinnamon**
1 1/4 tsp. **Baking powder**

Instructions:

Since the preparation of these cookies is very fast and easy, you can start by heating the oven at 180° C/ 356° F.

Next, cut the apples in pieces, remove their seeds, and grind them. Alternatively, you can use a kitchen chopper, if you wish to make the process easier.

Now simply mix all ingredients in a large bowl, and blend until the dough is fully homogenous.

Take a baking pan and cover it with baking paper.

Scoop some of the cookie dough and form small balls.

Place them in the tray and gently press them to shape them as traditional biscuits.

Bake for about 20 minutes until fully cooked.

Take them out of the oven and let them cool down completely.

Store in a sealed cookie jar for a few days (if they survive that long).

Gluten-free Oatmeal Cookies

Ingredients:

1 cup **Gluten-free fine oatmeal**
2 Tbsps. **Desiccated coconut**
1 tsp. **Cinnamon**
1 Tbsp. **Ground flax seeds**
20 **Dates** (pitted)
3 **Eggs**
3 Tbsps. **Coconut butter** (soft or melted)
1 cup **Milk** (cow, almond, rice, soy, etc.)
1 tsp. **Macca powder**
2 1/2 Tbsps. **Dark chocolate chips** (preferably sugar-free)

Instructions:

First, mix the oatmeal and the desiccated coconut with the milk, and leave them soak until they soften.

Next, place the eggs, the cinnamon, macca powder, the flax seeds, coconut butter, and the dates in a blender and mince them well.

Add the oatmeal and blend again until the mixture becomes fully homogenous.

Finally, add the chocolate chips and stir again (you can use the blender again or simply stir with a spoon).

If the mixture seems too liquid, add more oatmeal or some coconut flour (it is extremely absorbent).

While the cookie dough thickens, take a baking tray and cover it with baking paper; start heating the oven to 160° C/ 320° F (use the fan-assist option, if you have it).

Start scooping some of the cookie dough with a spoon and form small balls and place them on the baking tray.

Bake the biscuits for about 20 minutes until they get a nice golden crust at the top.

Remember to store them in a cookie jar once they cool down completely!

Enjoy!

Banana Cookies

Ingredients:

1/2 cup **Butter** (soft)
2 **Bananas** (ripe)
1/2 cup **Dates** (pitted)
1/2 cup **Chickpea flour**
1 cup **Rice flour**
1 Tbsp. **Cinnamon**
1 tsp. **Baking powder**
3 Tbsps. **Ground flax seeds**
2-3 Tbsps. **Dark chocolate chips** (preferably sugar-free)

Instructions:

Simply blend all ingredients completely in a kitchen robot (a blender, or a chopper).

The final result should be nice non-sticky cookie dough.

If not, add some more rice flour and blend again.

Next, you can start heating the oven to 170° C/338° F.

After that, take a baking tray and cover it with baking paper.

Form the biscuits as usual – shape them as small balls and press to make them flatter.

Bake the desserts for about 12-15 minutes. If you like them crunchier, leave them to get a nice golden crust at the top.

Voila!

"Fluffy" Coconut Cookies

Ingredients:

2 **Eggs**
1/2 cup **Pumpkin seed tahini** (or any other type you like)
3 Tbsps. **Date molasses**
2 Tbsps. **Coconut butter** (soft)
3 Tbsps. **Desiccated coconut**
2 Tbsps. **Coconut flour**
1/2 tsp. **Cinnamon**
1 tsp. **Baking soda**

Instructions:

Start by heating the oven to 160° C/ 320° F.

Next, simply blend all ingredients until they form nice homogenous sticky dough.

Scoop from the batter with a spoon, form small cookie balls, and place them in a baking tray covered with baking paper.

Bake the biscuits for about 10 minutes. You can use the fan-assist function of your oven, if it has one.

OTHER DELICIOUS GLUTEN-FREE DESSERTS

Petit Fours

Ingredients:

For the base:
2 **Eggs**
4 1/2 Tbsps. **Coconut sugar**
1 1/2 cup **Gluten free flour mix of choice**
1 Tbsp. **Carob powder** (or cocoa powder)
1 cup **Yogurt**
1/2 tsp. **Baking soda**
2 Tbsps. **Coconut butter** (soft)
1 tsp. **Vanilla extract**
1 **Lemon** (bio)

For the syrup:
1 cup **Nut milk** (coconut, almond, etc.)
Maple syrup – to taste

For the cream:
1 1/2 cup **Sour cream**
1 cup **Mascarpone**
1 **Banana**
Maple syrup – to taste
Dark chocolate flakes - optional

Instructions:

First, we start with the base for our petit fours.

Mix the yogurt with the baking soda and leave it for a bit to start frothing.

In the meantime, beat the eggs along with the sugar.

Next, add the bubbly yogurt, the butter, and blend them well.

Consecutively, add the dry ingredients – the flour, carob powder, and the vanilla extract.

Grate the zest of the lemon and add it to the mix.

Blend the batter well with a hand blender or a mixer.

Take a flat baking pan and cover it with baking paper.

Bake the "cake" in a preheated oven (at 180° C/ 356° F) until fully cooked (to a clean toothpick).

In the meantime, we can start making the cream.

Squeeze the juice from the lemon and mash the banana.

Mix the sour cream, the mascarpone, and blend them with a whisk.

Add the lemon juice, the banana puree, some maple syrup, and stir well once again. Remember that you are not obliged to add all the lemon juice. If you do not wish the cream to be sour, add less of it.

When the base for the desserts is ready, leave it for a bit while you make the juicy sweet syrup.

Simply warm the milk and mix it with the sweetener.

Pour the syrup on the cake and leave it to cool down completely.

Next, spread the cream on top and sprinkle the chocolate flakes, if you decide to include them.

Place the cake in the fridge to stiffen, and cut it in squares right before consumption.

Bon Appetite!

Coconut Petit Fours

Ingredients:

For the base:
2 **Eggs**
3 1/2 Tbsps. **Date molasses** (or date paste)
1 cup **Water** (warm)
3 Tbsps. **Coconut butter** (melted)
4 Tbsps. **Coconut flour**
3 Tbsps. **Coconut shreds** (full-fat)
1/2 tsp. **Baking soda**
1/4 tsp. **Apple cider vinegar**
A pinch of **Salt**

For the fruit jam:
2 cups **Fruits of choice** (without any seeds or pits)
1/4 tsp. **Cinnamon**
2 Tbsps. **Honey**
Some **Water** – to cover the fruits

Instructions:

First, we will start by making the jam.

Cut the fruits in medium pieces, place them in a metal pot, cover them with the water, add the cinnamon, and heat them on low temperature.

Let the mixture simmer and wait for some of the water to evaporate. When the jam has reached the desired consistency, take the pot off the heat and let it cool down.

When the sweet mass cools off below body temperature, add the honey, and stir to melt it and distribute it evenly.

Now we can move to the base of our petit fours.

At this point you can start heating the oven to 170° C/338° F.

Mix the date molasses with the warm water in a blender and leave it to soak for a bit.

If you are using hard date paste, cut it in small pieces before putting it in the blender.

Next, blend until the sweet mixture becomes homogeneous.

Consecutively, beat the eggs in a bowl, add the blended dates, the coconut butter, and stir well.

In another container, mix the flour, the baking soda, and the coconut shreds.

Transfer this mixture to the main batter and blend again.

Next, take a flat baking pan and cover it with baking paper.

Pour the cake mixture in and bake for about 15-20 minutes in the pre-heated oven.

Next, when the cake is fully cooked, take it out of the furnace, and leave it to cool down completely.

Cover the base of the petit fours with the fruit jam and cut the dessert in squares!

Enjoy!

Gluten-free Macarons

Ingredients:

For the macarons:
1/2 cup **Raw almonds**
3 Tbsps. **Almond flour**
3 Tbsps. **Coconut flour**
4 **Egg whites**
1 Tbsp. **Stevia***

For the cream:
1/2 cup **Dark chocolate** (preferably sugar-free)*
3-4 Tbsps. **Butter** (soft)
3-4 Tbsps. **Date molasses** (or ground dates)

Instructions:

First, grind the almonds in a kitchen chopper.

Next, mix them with the almond flour and the coconut flour. Stir well to blend them.

In another cup, beat the egg whites until stiff, and add the stevia extract.

Continue to whisk the whites until they blend with the sweetener.

Next, add the dry ingredients and gently stir to homogenize the mixture.

Start heating the oven to 160° C - 170° C (320° F - 338° F).

Now pour the batter in your favorite macaron mold using a piping bag.

Bake the desserts for about 10-15 minutes (or until fully cooked with a nice golden crust).

In the meantime, melt the chocolate in a double boiler, and blend it with the butter and the date molasses. Feel free to adjust the sweetness of the cream by changing the quantity of the dates.

When everything is ready and cooled down, assemble the macarons by spreading some of the cream between two semi-spheres and voila!

*The quantity of the stevia will depend on the type of product you use. Most extracts have a ratio to sugar as follows:

1 cup sugar = 1 tsp. liquid or powdered stevia

1 Tbsp. sugar = 1/4 tsp. powdered (6-9 drops liquid stevia)

1 tsp. sugar = a pinch of powdered (2-4 drops liquid stevia)

Keep in mind that there are other types of stevia extracts with different ratios, for example 1:1.

Eventually, experiment and see what quantities suit your taste best!

*If you do not have sugar-free chocolate at your disposal, you can always make it on your own! You can find two of my favorite healthy chocolate recipes in my FREE ebook "12 Healthy Dessert Recipes"

Energy Bars – 3 Variations

Ingredients:

For the base "dough":
1 cup **Peanut butter**
1 cup **Coconut butter**
1 cup **Almond flour**
1 cup **Coconut flour**
1 cup **Gluten-free oat bran** (or flax seed flour)
1 cup **Almond milk**

For variation 1:
2 Tbsps. **Peanut butter**
Some **Ground peanuts**

For variation 2:
1 Tbsp. **Matcha powder**
Some **Goji berries** (dry)

For variation 3:
Several **Dates to taste** (pitted)
Several **Dry apricots**
1 Tbsp. **Cocoa powder**
1 Tbsp. **Carob powder**
Stevia extract* – to taste
1 Tbsp. **Coconut butter**

Instructions:

First, we start preparing the base mixture for the energy bars.

Mix the peanut butter and the coconut butter and melt them in a double boiler.

Next, add the remaining ingredients for the "dough" and blend well. If you need to, adjust the quantities of the dry and liquid parts to reach the desired pliable consistency.

Divide the dough in three equal parts.

For the first variation, add the peanut butter to one part of the mixture and blend it nicely. Melt the peanut butter beforehand, if you wish to smoothen the process.

Next, roll out the dough at about 1 cm (0.4") and decorate with the ground peanuts. Place it in the freezer to tighten for several hours and cut it in the desired shapes.

For the second variation, take another part of the base mixture and mix it with the Matcha powder. Blend well and roll it out just like the first one.

Sprinkle some goji berries on top and put it in the freezer to keep its shape. Next, cut in the desired forms.

For the last variation, melt the coconut butter and place it in the blender. Add the remaining ingredients and blend well until you reach a homogenous paste.

Note: if the mixture becomes too dry and difficult to blend, add some water or milk.

Combine it with the base dough and mix well.

Finally, the last part is the same as the previous variations – roll the mixture out, and store in the freezer for a couple of hours. Next, cut in the desired shapes.

*The quantity of the stevia will depend on the type of product you use. Most extracts have a ratio to sugar as follows:

1 cup sugar = 1 tsp. liquid or powdered stevia

1 Tbsp. sugar = 1/4 tsp. powdered (6-9 drops liquid stevia)

1 tsp. sugar = a pinch of powdered (2-4 drops liquid stevia)

Keep in mind that there are other types of stevia extracts with different ratios, for example 1:1.

Eventually, experiment and see what quantities suit your taste best!

Coconut Bars

Ingredients:

6 **Egg whites**
2 **Egg yolks**
1 cup **Apricots**
1 1/2 cup **Desiccated coconut**
1/2 tsp. **Olive oil** (butter, coconut butter, etc.)
Decoration according your taste – **ground nuts, fruits, superfoods**, etc.

Instructions:

First, cut the apricots in small pieces.

If you do not have fresh fruits at the moment, you can use dried apricots (not treated with sugar or chemicals).

Simply soak them in some water or juice until they soften, and mince them in pieces.

Next, blend the egg whites, the yolks, apricots, and the desiccated coconut in a kitchen robot, a chopper, or a blender.

Take a flat baking pan, cover it with baking paper, and spread the oil on top of it to prevent the batter from sticking to it.

Now you can start heating the oven to 120° C- 130° C / 248° F - 266° F.

Pour the coconut mixture in the baking pan, decorate it with whatever you desire, and cook for about 10-15 minutes in the pre-heated oven.

When the dessert is ready and cooled down, cut it in the desired shapes.

Enjoy!

Protein Truffles

Ingredients:

3 1/2 Tbsps. **Cocoa butter**
3 1/2 Tbsps. **Maple syrup**
3 Tbsps. **Cocoa powder**
4 Tbsps. **Whey protein**
1 tsp. **Cinnamon**

Instructions:

First, we need to melt the cocoa butter. (You can do this step before measuring the 3 1/2 tablespoons. Alternatively, you can scoop out the quantity directly from the container.)

Place the cocoa butter chunks in a double boiler and heat them until they melt down.

Next, add the maple syrup and stir well to blend them.

Add the whey protein and 2 1/2 Tbsps. cocoa powder as well, and mix again to reach a homogenous paste.

Form small balls and cover them with the remaining cocoa powder.

Finally, place the truffles in a container and transfer them in the fridge for 1-2 hours to stiffen a bit.

Protein Dessert

Ingredients:

2 **Eggs**
1/2 cup **Cottage cheese** (curd)
2 Tbsps. **Coconut flour**
1 Tbsp. **Coconut butter** (soft)
1 tsp. **Vanilla extract**
3-4 Tbsps. **Berries of choice** (blueberries, raspberries, strawberries)
1-2 tsps. **Honey**

Instructions:

Start heating the oven to 170° C/338° F.

Next, simply blend all ingredients well (except the fruits) in a kitchen chopper, a robot, or a blender.

Consecutively, pour the mixture in a flat baking mold and cover it with the berries.

Bake the desserts for about 30 minutes. It is best to use the fan-assist function of the oven, if you have one.

Voila!

Cocoa Dessert with Plums

Ingredients:

1 cup **Cottage cheese**

5 1/2 Tbsps. **Ground raw almonds** (or blanched)

5 **Egg whites**

1 1/2 Tbsp. **Cocoa powder**

1 1/2 cup **Plums**

Some **Almonds** (for decoration) - optional

Some **Butter** (for the baking pan)

Instructions:

First, place the cottage cheese, the almonds, egg whites, and the cocoa powder in a blender (or a kitchen robot) and blend them well.

When the mixture becomes fully homogeneous, pit the plums and cut them in halves.

You can start heating the oven to 180° C/ 356° F.

Next, take a baking pan (with about 7"-8" diameter) and cover it with butter.

Now arrange the plums in the pan with their insides at the bottom of the container.

Consecutively, pour the batter in the pan and bake for about 40 minutes until fully cooked. You can use the fan-assist option of your oven, if you have it.

Finally, leave the dessert to cool down and flip it upside down in a large plate.

Decorate with some almonds, if you desire!

Coconut Crumble

Ingredients:

1/2 cup **Eggs**
1 cup **Rice flour**
1 cup **Gluten-free oatmeal** (ground)
1/2 cup **Almond flour**
1 tsp. **Baking powder**
1/2 cup **Desiccated coconut**
1 cup **Coconut butter** (hard)
2 cups **Blackberries**
1 cup **Blueberries**
1 Tbsp. **Lemon juice**
1 tsp. (heaped) **Apple pectin**

Instructions:

Start by heating the oven to 170° C/338° F.

Next, take a square baking pan (about 7" x 7"), cover it with some olive oil and baking paper. Alternatively, you can use a rectangular pan without any problem.

In a large bowl, mix the dry ingredients – the rice flour, almond flour, baking powder, the sugar (leave 2 Tbsps. for the fruits), oatmeal, and the coconut shreds.

Next, add the coconut butter, and start mashing the mixture with a fork.

In another container, mix the fruits with two tablespoons of the sugar, the lemon juice, and the apple pectin.

Blend the sweet mixture well and add it to the main dough.

Transfer the mass to the baking pan and cook for about 40 minutes (until the dessert gets a nice golden crust at the top).

Chocolate Chia Pudding

Ingredients:

1 1/2 cup **Milk**
1/3 cup **Chia**
1/4 cup **Cocoa powder**
1/2 tsp. **Cinnamon**
1/4 tsp. **Salt** (sea or Himalayan)
10 **Dates** (pitted)

Instructions:

Simply place all ingredients in a blender and stir well.

When the mixture becomes fully homogenous, pour it in small dessert cups and place them in the fridge.

Cool the pudding for several hours or overnight to tighten.

Enjoy!

My notes:

Raspberry Panna Cotta

Ingredients:

2 cups **Cooking cream** (20% fat)
1/2 cup **Milk**
4 tsps. **Gelatin**
Some **Water** – for the gelatin
Maple syrup – to taste
1 cup **Raspberries**

Instructions:

Cover the gelatin with some water and wait for it to start bulging.

In the meantime, take half of the raspberries and 1 tablespoon of the maple syrup and heat them in low temperature.

Blend them with a hand blender and let the fruits simmer for a bit.

Next, strain the sweet syrup from the seeds and leave it aside to cool down.

Meanwhile, mix the cooking cream, the milk, and the remaining maple syrup in a metal pot, and heat them as well. When the dairy products blend completely, take them off the heat.

Next, add a little bit more water to the gelatin and heat it in a double boiler.

Stir until it melts and becomes transparent.

Now take 2 tablespoons of the gelatin and mix them with the raspberry syrup.

Blend the remaining of it (the gelatin) with the dairy mixture.

Finally, is it time to assemble the panna cottas.

Take some dessert cups (or muffin molds) and place 1-2 tablespoons of the raspberry syrup in each one of them.

Place them in the freezer for several minutes for the raspberry jelly to stiffen.

Now fill the cups with the cream and place them in the fridge for the gelatin to do its magic!

Bon Appetite!

Cocoa Soufflé with Cottage Cheese

Ingredients:

1 cup **Cottage cheese** (or ricotta)
1/2 cup **Milk**
1 1/2 Tbsp. **Gelatin**
1 cup **Water**
2 Tbsps. **Cocoa powder**
2 Tbsps. **Maple syrup** (agave, coconut sugar, etc.)

Instructions:

If your cottage cheese is cold from the fridge, take it out to warm up to room temperature.

Mix the water and the gelatin in a metal pot, and leave it for about half an hour to bulge.

Next, add the cocoa powder, the maple syrup, the milk, and heat the mixture on low temperature. You can always adjust the quantity of the sweetener to your taste!

Stir continuously until the cocoa and the gelatin are fully melted.

Next, add the cottage cheese, stir, and blend with a hand blender until you reach a homogenous mass.

Pour the mixture in suitable dessert cups and place them in the fridge for at least 2 hours (or overnight) to stiffen.

Pumpkin Doughnuts

Ingredients:

1/2 cup **Pumpkin** (boiled or steamed)
2 **Eggs**
2 Tbsps. **Sour cream**
1/2 tsp. **Baking powder**
1 Tbsp. (heaped) **Coconut flour**
1/2 tsp. **Coconut butter** (soft)
1 tsp. **Vanilla extract**
Some **Diced Prunes and apples** – optional
Some **Desiccated coconut** - optional

Instructions:

The preparation of the doughnuts is very simple.

Simply blend all ingredients well until you reach a homogeneous mass.

If you wish to add more fiber and make them crunchier, add some diced prunes and apples, and some coconut shreds.

Pour the batter in your doughnut maker and bake until they get a nice golden crust.

If you do not have a doughnut maker, feel free to experiment with waffles or pancakes!

Sweet Rice Semolina Meal

Ingredients:

1/2 cup **Rice semolina**
2 cups **Milk** (cow or vegan)
2 Tbsps. **Butter**
Some **Sweetener of choice** (maple syrup, agave, stevia*, etc.) – to taste
Some **Cinnamon** – for decoration

Instructions:

First, start melting the butter in a metal pot on low temperature.

Next, add the semolina, stir well, and wait for it to absorb all of the butter.

Consecutively, slowly and gently start adding the milk in a thin stream while continue stirring the mixture.

Finally, add the sweetener and blend the mixture until it reaches the desired consistency.

Now take a dessert cup (or cups) and moist them on the inside. Pour the semolina meal and wait for it to cool down completely.

Turn the cup upside down to remove the dessert and sprinkle some cinnamon at the top.

That's it! Easy-peasy!

*The quantity of the stevia will depend on the type of product you use. Most extracts have a ratio to sugar as follows:

1 cup sugar = 1 tsp. liquid or powdered stevia

1 Tbsp. sugar = 1/4 tsp. powdered (6-9 drops liquid stevia)

1 tsp. sugar = a pinch of powdered (2-4 drops liquid stevia)

Keep in mind that there are other types of stevia extracts with different ratios, for example 1:1.

Eventually, experiment and see what quantities suit your taste best!

My notes:

Thank you!

I want to thank you for purchasing this book and reading it all the way to the end. I hope it has been helpful and informative. If you liked this volume, you can support my work and make it more visible for others who are looking for this kind of knowledge! I would deeply appreciate if you take a minute and write a short review on Amazon. I thank you in advance for your support!
Kind regards and best wishes,
Milica

P.S. And don't forget to get your free ebooks:
"10 Powerful Immune Boosting Recipes"
"12 Healthy Dessert Recipes"
"15 Delicious & Healthy Smoothies"
"The Complete Ayurveda Detox"

Go to *www.MindBodyAndSpiritWellbeing.com* and claim your gifts!

Or simply scan the QR code below:

About the author

Milica Vladova dedicated her work to spread the valuable knowledge of the physical, emotional, and spiritual wellbeing. She is determined to make the world healthier, happier, and more successful!

Her works have been published on *The Huffington Post*, *Thrive Global*, *The Elephant Journal*, *Sivana Spirit*, *YogiApproved*, *Steven Aitchison*, and more.

Find her on:
http://mindbodyandspiritwellbeing.com
https://facebook.com/**mindbodyandspiritwellbeing**
https://www.pinterest.com/**milicavladova**
https://twitter.com/**Holistic_Milky**

Milica is also the author of:

Complete Body Cleansing and Strong Immunity Bundle

- **Healthy recipes** with white sugar and white flour alternatives!
- Plenty of toning, refreshing, and cleansing **smoothie recipes!**
- Detoxing and strengthening aromatic **herbal blends!**
- Loads of delicious **immune boosting recipes** and remedies.
- Which exercises can help us **expel more toxins** from our cells;
- **Simple weekly, monthly, and annual detox rituals** to help you boost your energy, lose weight naturally, fight chronic fatigue, and prevent from diseases.
- How to purify your system **without starving?**
- How to **deeply detox and heal your colon, liver, kidneys, lungs, lymph**, and more?
- How to naturally **get rid of parasites?**
- **Healthy gut - healthy you!** How to take care of our beneficial colon bacteria?
- **Natural probiotics and prebiotics** - how to make them at home with natural ingredients?
- **Adaptogens** - the key to dealing with stress, infertility and building our strong immunity.
- Natural ways and systems to **prevent, stop, and heal from cancer** cell formation.
- **The best herbs, essential oils and homeopathic remedies** to prevent from diseases, viruses, fungi, and bacteria.
- and much more!

★★★★★**Science mixed with love for a winning combo**

What a wealth of information filled with knowledge and innate insight into how the body functions and heals. So many great choices offered. These books are wonderful at dipping into every day for fresh ideas. Just applying some of the knowledge is still so powerful at helping you get fit and healthy from the inside out. Great recipes and full of science mixed with genuine love from the author.

~ Reviewer on Amazon.com

★★★★★**Accessible, clear, and gently written**

I wish all health books were written this way!

First, Ms. Vladova shares exhaustive information on cleansing and eating well with such a gentle, non-judgemental attitude.

And she meets the reader where they are. For instance, after introducing the Weekly Fasting Day with just tea or Water, Ms. Vladova suggest that if that is too extreme for you at the beginning, you can start with a day of fasting that involves Green Smoothies instead. And if even that is too much, she offers a plan for a day with just rice and apples.

As someone who's never tried any cleanses, her approach was so accessible!

Second, there is NO FLUFF! She gets right into talking about how to eat better and cleanse your body.

Recipes are easy to understand and well explained.

~ J D on Amazon.com

★★★★★ **The Perfect Christmas Stocking Filler - A Recovery Programme for those who Overindulge**

Gosh, this is a must-buy for anyone who cares about their body.

I'd already had some great results from the Healthy Body Cleanse detox programme, but the other two books are an absolute bargain - so full of useful information to keep you on track.

Although it's a great Christmas pressie for those of us who have no willpower in the season of gross overindulgence, it's actually a great regime to follow in the month before to prepare your body for the onslaught.

A win-win either way.

~ **FireDancer on Amazon.com**

★★★★★ **A great resource!**

What a wonderful resource, so jam-packed with information! The body has a great mechanism to heal itself and these books help with that. I'm really pleased because my daily smoothies are now more interesting with the recipes included. The other recipes are easily adapted if you are vegan like I am. This bundle is what I would term a coffee-table book because once you've read it through you can dip into it every day or whenever you need to be reminded of the great info inside. My health has greatly improved and I recommend this bundle to anyone on the same journey to health or thinking about it.

~ **Karen Aminadra on Amazon.com**

DIY Homemade Beauty Products Bundle

MORE THAN 500 NATURAL ORGANIC BEAUTY RECIPES FOR THE WHOLE BODY!

What are you going to find in this book?
- Universal **face masks** for all skin types.
- **Lotions and cremes** for oily, dry, and mature skin.
- **Anti-aging and rejuvenating serums** for the face and eye contour.
- Natural **remedies for acne, pimples, blackheads**, etc.
- Gentle **whitening treatments** for brighter complexion and radiant skin.
- Universal nourishing **hair masks**;
- **Hair repair** recipes;
- **Anti-split ends** treatments;
- Natural **remedies for hair-loss** and thinning hair;
- **Hair growth** stimulators;
- **Dandruff healing masks** and ointments for oily and itchy scalp;
- **Herbal rinsing, organic shampoo recipes** and oil blends;
- Nourishing **body butters and lotions**;
- **Non-toxic sunscreen** recipes;
- Cleansing and healing **body scrubs and exfoliators**;
- **Anti-cellulite treatments** and massaging oils;
- Nourishing and **anti-aging hand cremes** and masks;
- **Nail strengthening** procedures;
- Natural **toothpastes and mouthwashes**;
- and more...

★★★★★Great deal!

This budle is a great resource for homemade beauty products! These are gentle and natural products!

~ **Kelly Phister on Amazon.com**

★★★★★Great set of books that has numerous recipes for everyone

Great set of books that has numerous recipes for every item.

The ingredients required are not difficult to come by. Overall a very nice and helpful set of books that comes in very handy for lotions and hand creams, hair masks etc. I recommend this book.

~ **Joanne Beal on Amazon.com**

★★★★★Start saving money and be healthier, too!

Talk about your natural resource for all things you purchase. Now I am the first one to tell people to stop buying prepare items like soap, shampoo and the like, and to make their own. I go to Lush religiously and purchase their items. It is all natural barring a few essential ingredients that are needed to preserve the products, and even them it is as gentle and natural as possible. Show yourself some love and get this book, and save yourself some money at Lush, because their products are not cheap and this DIY boom is loaded with so much and really is worth the small price investment as you will save literally thousands with all these recipes and all the imformation!

~ **Aisha Hashmi on Amazon.com**

The Healthy Vegan Recipes Cookbook

MORE THAN 80 HEALTHY VEGAN RECIPES FOR THE WHOLE FAMILY!

In this volume you will find:
- Healthy vegan **main course dishes**;
- **Bread and salty snacks** recipes.
- **Dips and side dishes.**
- Yummy **sugar-free desserts**.
- Interesting info about **the numerous benefits of vegan foods**. and more!

★★★★★**Perfect when you're in a pinch!**

I referred to this recipe book several times over the past week to get some healthy, tasty recipes for my vegan/vegetarian friends. The author definitely has first-hand experience preparing these dishes, provides clear tips and alternatives, and also imparts knowledge about the health benefits. I'm short, it's a practical recipe book, but it's also an insightful read. I'll be reaching for this book over the holiday season for more inspiration. I'm thinking of pulling together a raw nut loaf and I'm pretty sure I saw a recipe in here I could swing! I know it won't disappoint! (I'm considering purchasing a hard copy this Xmas for a raw food friend!)

~ **Cynthia Luna on Amazon.com**

★★★★★**Try these recipes!**

Lots of wonderful recipes that I cannot wait to try. Healthy and nutritious meals! Snacks!

~ **Aisha Hashmi on Amazon.com**

Printed in Great Britain
by Amazon